FEROCITY

Navigating Future Careers
Through Halo Skills

NALIN KUMAR SINGH

ISBN 979-8-89415-377-3

Contents

PART 2

Skills For Future Careers — 63

PART 3

Future Jobs & Careers   127

PART 4

Job Readiness   153

Foreword

In the dynamic landscape of the modern job market, the quest for relevance and excellence is unending. *Ferocity: Navigating Future Careers through Halo Skills*, authored by my long-time friend and esteemed colleague, Nalin K. Singh, emerges as a beacon of insight in this complex world. Over the past four decades, I have witnessed Nalin's extraordinary journey, marked by rich experiences, deep knowledge, and an unwavering commitment to excellence.

Nalin's professional odyssey spans over thirty years, during which he has donned various hats – from a visionary leader in Fortune 500 companies to a mentor who has shaped the futures of countless individuals. His profound understanding of industries, corporate dynamics, and interpersonal relationships, combined with an innate cultural competence honed through his work in diverse countries, sets him apart as an authority in his field. It is this very expertise that he brings to the table in *Ferocity*.

Beyond the corporate arena, Nalin's creativity and versatility shine through his varied endeavours as a filmmaker and a prolific writer. His contributions to the discourse on education and skilling have been especially impactful, resonating with a wide spectrum of audiences. This blend of diverse experiences has endowed him with a deep understanding of the evolving job landscape.

This book, Nalin's eighth publication and fourth in the business genre, delves into what he terms 'Halo Skills' – a groundbreaking concept that redefines the skill set necessary for thriving in future job markets. The term 'Halo Skills' is not just a buzzword; it encapsulates a new dimension of professional capabilities that transcend traditional boundaries. These skills are about embracing adaptability, creativity, and a holistic approach to problem-solving – elements that are becoming increasingly vital in our fast-paced, technology-driven world.

"Ferocity" is not merely a guide; it is a roadmap to navigating the unpredictable terrains of future employment landscapes. The book meticulously dissects the evolving nature of work, the shifting paradigms of employment, and the new rules of the corporate game. It's a testament to Nalin's belief that the future belongs to those who are prepared to embrace change, challenge norms, and step beyond their comfort zones.

One of the most compelling aspects of this book is its practical approach. Nalin does not just theorise about future skills; he provides actionable strategies and real-life examples that resonate with professionals at all levels. His narrative is enriched with anecdotes from his extensive career, offering readers a glimpse into the practical application of these Halo Skills in various global scenarios.

Moreover, Nalin's writing style is engaging and accessible, making complex concepts easy to grasp. He has a unique ability to connect with his readers, drawing them into a conversation rather than a lecture. This quality, I believe, is what sets "Ferocity" apart from other books in the genre.

In conclusion, "Ferocity: Navigating Future Careers through Halo Skills" is more than just a book; it's a mentor in print form. For professionals looking to stay ahead of the curve, for students aspiring to carve out successful careers, and for leaders seeking to foster a culture of innovation and resilience, this book is an indispensable resource. Nalin K. Singh, through his vast experience and insightful perspectives, has crafted a work that is destined to become a cornerstone in the library of future skills and professional development.

Sachin V. Gopalan

Impact Oriented Serial Entrepreneur

Jakarta, Indonesia

Part 1

MODERN LEARNING & CAREER LANDSCAPE

"Universities offer education,
but life delivers the true lessons."

The Unholy Quaternity: Fear, Focus, Desire, and Velocity – Imperative for Future Job Success

"In the future job market, those who harness fear, maintain laser-like focus, fuel their journey with relentless desire, and adapt with unmatched velocity will be the architects of their own unprecedented success."

The only constant is change in the dynamic world of the job market. The formula for success is undergoing a radical transformation. As we hurtle into the future, the amalgamation of fear, focus, desire, and velocity emerges as the unholy quaternity that propels individuals towards unprecedented success in the jobs of tomorrow.

Fear, often deemed a negative emotion, is a powerful catalyst when harnessed appropriately. The fear of stagnation, irrelevance, and obscurity can be the driving force behind the relentless pursuit of knowledge and innovation. In the job market of the future, where industries will rise and fall at the blink of an eye, those who are paralysed by the fear of falling behind will be left in the dust.

Consider fear as the wake-up call, the primal instinct that jolts one into action. Fear, when converted into fuel, becomes the energy that propels individuals to stay ahead of the curve. The fear of automation rendering jobs obsolete or being outshone by artificial intelligence ignites the fire of resilience and adaptability. To succeed in the jobs of the future, individuals must embrace fear as a companion rather than an adversary, using it to stay vigilant, agile, and ready to pivot when necessary.

Focus, the unwavering concentration on a singular goal, is the linchpin that separates the successful from the mediocre. In an era where distractions abound, the ability to zero in on a specific task or skill set is not just an asset but a prerequisite. The jobs of the future demand specialists, not generalists, individuals who can delve deep into a subject, dissect its intricacies, and emerge as masters in their domain.

Consider focus as the laser beam cutting through the fog of ambiguity. In an age where information overload is the norm, the capacity to filter out the noise and concentrate on what truly matters is invaluable. It is the focused mind that can navigate the complexities of evolving industries, deciphering patterns and predicting trends that elude the distracted.

Desire, the burning hunger for success, is the intangible force that propels individuals to push boundaries and surpass limits. In the jobs of the future, where innovation is the currency of progress, those who are content with mediocrity will be relegated to the sidelines. The insatiable desire to create, innovate, and excel is the driving force that distinguishes the game-changers from the bystanders.

Consider desire as the relentless engine powering progress. In the dynamic job market of the future, complacency is the enemy. The desire to excel, to contribute meaningfully, and to leave an indelible mark on one's field is the magnet that attracts success. It is the force that transforms challenges into opportunities and setbacks into stepping stones.

Velocity, the speed and direction of one's actions, is the final piece of the puzzle. In a world where agility is the currency of survival, the ability to adapt and move swiftly is non-negotiable. The jobs of the future will not wait for the hesitant; they belong to those who can ride the wave of change with unparalleled velocity.

Consider velocity as the accelerator pedal in the race for success. In an era where industries evolve at breakneck speed, those who can keep pace with change will emerge victorious. The rapid adoption of new technologies, methodologies, and approaches is not a luxury but a necessity. The velocity with which one can learn, unlearn, and relearn will determine their relevance in the job market of the future.

The synergy of fear, focus, desire, and velocity forms the cornerstone of success in the jobs of the future. It is not a mere concoction of motivational buzzwords but a strategic roadmap for navigating the unpredictable terrain that lies ahead. Those who dismiss these elements as ephemeral trends do so at their own peril, for they are the pillars upon which the future of work rests.

To succeed in the jobs of the future, individuals must first confront and embrace their fears. Fear, when acknowledged and utilised as a source of motivation, becomes the impetus for continuous learning and growth. The fear of technological obsolescence should drive individuals to upskill and reskill, ensuring that they remain indispensable in a landscape where automation is the norm.

Focus is the antidote to the scattergun approach that many adopt in their professional lives. The jobs of the future will demand specialists who can contribute unique insights and expertise to their respective fields. Individuals must resist the temptation to spread themselves thin, instead honing in on a specific skill set or knowledge domain. It is the focused mind that can delve into the nuances of a subject, unlocking innovations that elude the unfocused.

Desire is the invisible force that sets the extraordinary apart from the ordinary. The jobs of the future require individuals who are not content with the status quo but are driven by an unquenchable thirst for success. It is the burning desire to make a difference, to leave a lasting legacy, that fuels the relentless pursuit of excellence. Those who lack this intrinsic motivation may find themselves relegated to the sidelines as the pace of progress accelerates.

Velocity, the ability to adapt and move swiftly, is the final and perhaps the most crucial element in the formula for success. In an era where change is the only constant, the ability to pivot and embrace new technologies and methodologies is paramount. The jobs of the future will belong to those who can keep pace with the rapid evolution of industries. Individuals must cultivate a mindset of continuous learning, unlearning, and relearning to navigate the ever-shifting landscape of the future job market.

The unholy quaternity of fear, focus, desire, and velocity is not a mere aspirational concept but a pragmatic approach to thriving in the jobs of the future. Those who can harness the power of fear as a motivational force, maintain an unwavering focus on their goals, cultivate an insatiable desire for success, and move with unparalleled velocity in the face of change will not only survive but thrive in the dynamic landscape that lies ahead. It is a clarion call for individuals to embrace these elements, for they are the keys to unlocking a future where success is not just achieved but sustained.

The Evolution of Self: Passion, Purpose, and Identity in Individual Journeys

"From the sparks of passion to the guiding light of purpose, our evolving identities form a legacy that weaves through the fabric of human existence."

Human existence is a complex tapestry woven with threads of passion, purpose, and identity. These elements form the essence of our being, shaping our individual journeys and influencing the dynamics of our relationships. The trajectory from passion to purpose and, eventually, identity is a fascinating exploration of self-discovery and personal growth. In this article, we delve into the profound evolution of individuals and relationships as they navigate the intricate pathways of passion, purpose, and identity.

The Ignition of Passion

Passion serves as the catalyst for many significant beginnings. It is the fiery force that ignites the spark in individuals and relationships, setting the stage for exploration and discovery. In the early stages

of life or a relationship, passion manifests itself in various forms –
be it a burning desire for personal achievements, creative pursuits,
or the intense emotions that characterise romantic entanglements.

Personal passion often emerges in the pursuit of one's interests,
talents, and dreams. Whether it's a budding artist experimenting
with colours on a canvas or an aspiring scientist delving into the
mysteries of the universe, the initial connection to passion is deeply
personal. It fuels the desire to excel and to find fulfilment in one's
chosen endeavours.

As individuals immerse themselves in their passions, they
experience a sense of purpose and direction. The energy derived
from pursuing what one loves provides the motivation to overcome
obstacles and challenges. Passion becomes a driving force, pushing
individuals to refine their skills, broaden their knowledge, and
reach new heights.

In relationships, passion often manifests as the euphoria of
newfound love. The early stages of romantic connections are
characterised by intense emotions, heightened excitement, and
a magnetic pull toward each other. Shared interests and mutual
passions can create a strong bond, fostering a sense of unity and
connection.

However, the ebullient flames of passion can be unpredictable.
They may burn brightly in the beginning, but sustaining that
intensity requires effort, understanding, and adaptation.
Relationships that endure recognise the need for a deeper
foundation beyond initial passion, transitioning into a quest for
shared purpose.

The Quest for Purpose

While passion sets the stage, purpose provides the script for a meaningful and fulfilling life. As individuals and relationships mature, the focus often shifts from the thrill of passion to a more profound search for purpose – a reason for being that goes beyond personal satisfaction.

Discovering personal purpose involves aligning one's passions with a broader sense of meaning and contribution to the world. It requires introspection, self-awareness, and a willingness to explore the deeper facets of one's existence. Whether it's through a career, creative pursuits, or philanthropy, individuals seek to make a positive impact and find fulfilment in their chosen paths.

"The pursuit of purpose may lead individuals to confront challenges and make sacrifices. It often involves a process of self-discovery, where individuals assess their values, strengths, and aspirations. The realisation of purpose can bring a sense of direction, resilience in the face of adversity, and a profound connection to something greater than oneself.

In relationships, the transition from passion to purpose involves the evolution of shared goals and values. Couples move beyond the initial excitement of being together and embark on a journey to build a life that aligns with their collective aspirations. This shared purpose becomes the driving force that sustains the relationship through trials and tribulations.

Couples may discover purpose in raising a family, contributing to their community, or pursuing shared passions and projects. The ability to communicate and compromise becomes crucial as individuals navigate the intersection of their personal purposes within the context of a relationship. The synergy between individual and shared purposes forms the bedrock of a lasting and fulfilling partnership."

The Search for Identity

"As individuals and relationships establish a sense of purpose, the natural progression leads to the exploration of identity. Identity encompasses not only how we perceive ourselves but also how we are perceived by others – within our families, communities, and societies at large. It involves the creation of a legacy that extends beyond our lifetime.

The quest for individual identity involves a deep understanding of one's values, beliefs, and unique qualities. It is a continuous process of self-discovery and self-expression, requiring the courage to embrace authenticity. Individuals often grapple with questions of identity, seeking to align their actions with their core values and leave a positive mark on the world.

Identity is not static; it evolves with life experiences, personal growth, and the acquisition of wisdom. It may involve breaking free from societal expectations, pursuing unconventional paths, and embracing one's true self. The pursuit of individual identity is a lifelong journey that contributes to personal fulfillment and a sense of purpose beyond the self.

In relationships, the quest for identity involves balancing the individuality of each partner with the unity of the partnership. Couples navigate the delicate dance of maintaining a sense of self while intertwining their lives. The ability to respect and support each other's individual identities strengthens the foundation of the relationship.

As relationships mature, couples often find ways to contribute to each other's personal growth and identity. They become each other's pillars of support, encouraging exploration and self-expression. The shared identity of a couple extends beyond the individuals, creating a unique narrative that forms the basis of their legacy.

Leaving a Lasting Legacy

The culmination of a life well-lived involves leaving a lasting legacy – a mark on the world that outlives the individual. Legacy encompasses the impact individuals have on their families, communities, and the broader societal tapestry. It is the final chapter in the intricate interplay between passion, purpose, and identity.

Individuals aspire to leave a legacy that reflects their values and contributions. This may manifest in various forms, from groundbreaking achievements in a chosen field to acts of kindness and generosity that ripple through communities. The pursuit of a meaningful legacy is often motivated by the desire to be remembered for making a positive difference in the world.

The legacy-building process may involve passing on knowledge, values, and traditions to future generations. It can also be expressed through creative works, innovations, or philanthropic efforts. Ultimately, an individual's legacy is the imprint they leave on the collective memory of those whose lives they touched.

In relationships, the legacy extends beyond the individuals involved to encompass the impact on family, friends, and the community. The values and lessons shared within a partnership influence future generations, creating a legacy that transcends the temporal boundaries of individual lifetimes.

Couples who have navigated the journey from passion to purpose to identity often leave a legacy of resilience, love, and shared values. Their stories become a source of inspiration for others embarking on similar journeys, reinforcing the belief that enduring relationships and meaningful legacies are attainable through dedication and mutual growth.

The evolution from passion to purpose to identity is a profound and interconnected journey that shapes the essence of human existence. While passion serves as the initial spark, purpose becomes the guiding force that imbues life with meaning. The quest for identity completes the narrative, leaving a lasting legacy that echoes through time.

Individuals and relationships that successfully navigate this journey find fulfillment, resilience, and a sense of belonging. The interplay between passion, purpose, and identity weaves a rich tapestry that reflects the intricate beauty of the human experience. As we embark on our individual journeys and cultivate meaningful relationships, let us recognise the transformative power of passion, the purposeful drive that sustains us, and the enduring legacy that we leave behind for generations to come."

Industry 4.0: Why the Hullabaloo About Reskilling & Upskilling

"Navigating Industry 4.0 demands a profound re-evaluation of personal skills, driven by unprecedented technological integration and connectivity, setting it apart from all previous industrial revolutions."

"We are thrust into the heart of Industry 4.0, a time pulsating with the relentless rhythm of innovation and transformation! To navigate this era, one must arm themselves with skills and competencies that resonate with the demands of these electrifying times. I hail from the bustling metropolis of Bengaluru, a modern cityscape that thrives on progress. Yet, amidst this rapid advancement, I find a startling absence in my upbringing – conversations about personal skills in relation to the industrial revolutions were conspicuously missing.

Driven by an insatiable curiosity, I delved into the experiences of the generation before me, seeking answers. They, too, echoed my observations, confirming a striking contrast: there was no overt anxiety or discussion about aligning personal skills with the waves of Industry 1.0, 2.0, or 3.0. This realisation leads to an intriguing and burning question: What is it about Industry 4.0 that sets it apart, igniting a whirlwind of concern and urgency in everyone? Why does this particular era demand such a drastic re-evaluation of our skills and competencies? The answer lies somewhere in the dynamic, ever-evolving landscape of Industry 4.0 – a landscape that challenges us to adapt or be left behind in its dust!

Let us look at the four widely accepted Industrial revolutions and their impact.

1. First Industrial Revolution:
    - Time Period: Late 18th century to mid-19th century.
    - Key Advancements: Steam engine, mechanisation of textile production, and the use of water and steam power.
    - Impact: Shifted from agrarian economies to industrialised societies.

From a personal skilling perspective, there is not much change at a mass population level. A few people had to learn how to operate a steam engine and operate some mechanical equipment. Society at large was unaffected except for the convenience of a train or faster production times.

2. Second Industrial Revolution:
    - Time Period: Late 19th century to early 20th century.
    - Key Advancements: Electricity, the internal combustion engine, mass production, and the expansion of the railroads.
    - Impact: Introduced mass production, urbanisation, and increased economic and industrial growth.

Here, too, the impact is in pockets where the changes took place. Personally, I think you just enjoyed the benefits of electricity and probably needed to learn how to change a light bulb.

3. Third Industrial Revolution:

    - Time Period: Late 20th century.

    - Key Advancements: Electronics, the Internet, and automation.

    - Impact: The rise of digital technology, automation, and globalisation.

This is when mass upskilling and reskilling started. The advent of personal computers and mobile phones in the last few years of the 20th century meant that almost everyone had to learn how to use these devices.

4. The Fourth Industrial Revolution (Industry 4.0):

    - Time Period: Ongoing, starting around the late 20th century and continuing into the 21st century.

    - Key Advancements: Cyber-physical systems, the Internet of Things (IoT), artificial intelligence (AI), big data, 3D printing, and advanced robotics.

    - Impact: The convergence of physical and digital technologies, blurring the lines between the physical, digital, and biological worlds. Industry 4.0 is characterised by data-driven decision-making, increased connectivity, and the ability to customise products and services on a large scale.

The convergence of multiple technologies and the penetration of multiple devices in all aspects of our lives now require a high degree of digital and technological competency. Without the ability to use these connected devices and an understanding of their convergence, we just cannot function in modern society, let alone the workplace.

Industry 4.0 represents the Fourth Industrial Revolution, and it differs from earlier industrial revolutions (the first, second, and third) in several key ways:

Key Differences

1. Technology Integration: Industry 4.0 represents a tighter integration of digital technologies into the industrial process, enabling real-time data exchange and automation. This level of integration was not present in earlier industrial revolutions.

2. Data and Connectivity: Industry 4.0 relies heavily on data, sensors, and the internet to connect devices and systems. The first three revolutions primarily focused on mechanical and electrical advancements.

3. Customisation: Industry 4.0 enables a high degree of product and service customisation, thanks to technologies like 3D printing and data analytics. Previous revolutions were more centred on mass production.

4. Decentralisation: Industry 4.0 promotes decentralised decision-making and localised production through interconnected systems, whereas earlier industrial revolutions often relied on centralised factories.

5. Skills and Workforce: Industry 4.0 requires a highly skilled workforce capable of handling advanced technologies and data analysis, while earlier revolutions led to the growth of unskilled labour in many industries.

6. Sustainability: Industry 4.0 emphasises sustainability and resource efficiency more than previous revolutions, with a focus on reducing waste and energy consumption.

In summary, Industry 4.0 represents a fundamental shift in the way industries operate, with a strong focus on digital technologies, connectivity, and customisation. It builds on the advancements of earlier industrial revolutions but takes them to a new level by merging the physical and digital worlds.

Evolution of Skill Demand Through Industrial Generations and the Need for Continuous Skill Development

"Each industrial revolution has transformed not just the tools we use, but the very essence of the skills required, underscoring the perpetual need for adaptability and lifelong learning."

The landscape of required skills has undergone a significant transformation through the four industrial revolutions. While certain core skills remain vital, their application has evolved dramatically, mirroring the advancements in technology and societal changes. In this exploration, we will delve into how these skill demands have evolved and the imperative for continuous practice and enhancement of these skills.

1. *First Industrial Revolution (1760-1840): Craftsmanship to Mechanisation*

   Skill Shift: Manual labour and craftsmanship were the cornerstones of the first industrial era. Skills like weaving and metalworking were in high demand.

Evolution Example: The weaver's artistry, once a handcraft, adapted to the operation of mechanical looms.

Continuous Skill Development: Artisans had to evolve from manual craftsmanship to understanding and operating machinery, requiring continuous learning to stay relevant.

2. *Second Industrial Revolution (1870-1914):   Mechanisation to Mass Production*

Skill Shift: The advent of assembly lines and mass production shifted the skill focus to repetitive, process-oriented tasks.

Evolution Example: Assembly line workers replaced individual craftsmen, requiring less artisan skill but more coordination and speed.

Continuous Skill Development: Workers needed to adapt to faster-paced, more efficient production methods and learn to work in tandem with machines and other workers.

3. *Third Industrial Revolution (1960s-2000s):   Automation and Computerisation*

Skill Shift: The rise of automation and computers brought a demand for technical and digital literacy.

Evolution Example: Typists, who once used mechanical typewriters, transitioned to word processing on computers, necessitating digital literacy.

Continuous Skill Development: Professionals had to continually update their computer skills, learning new software and adapting to evolving technology.

Fourth Industrial Revolution (21st Century):   Digitalisation and Interconnectivity

Skill Shift: Advanced digital skills, data literacy, and AI familiarity have become crucial.

Evolution Example: Data analysis has evolved from manual number crunching to sophisticated use of AI and machine learning algorithms.

Continuous Skill Development: Today's workforce must engage in lifelong learning to keep pace with rapidly advancing technologies and methodologies.

The Necessity of Skill Practice and Honing

Beyond Acquisition: Merely acquiring a skill is no longer sufficient in the fast-paced, ever-evolving industrial landscape.

Practice and Adaptation: Skills need to be continuously practiced, honed, and adapted. This ongoing process ensures that professionals can not only keep up with current demands but also anticipate future changes.

Example: A software developer must constantly learn new programming languages and frameworks to remain effective and competitive.

The evolution of skill demands through the industrial generations highlights a consistent theme: the necessity of adapting and enhancing skills to meet the changing demands of the workplace. As we progress further into the Fourth Industrial Revolution, this need for continuous skill development and adaptation becomes even more pronounced, ensuring professionals remain competent and relevant in an ever-changing world.

Socio-Career Landscape & Timing

"In a world where the terrain of higher education is rapidly shifting, graduates must become agile navigators of an uncertain future, equipped with the skills and resilience to thrive amidst change."

As the landscape of higher education undergoes global disruptions, fresh graduates find themselves navigating an increasingly uncertain future. This uncertainty is amplified by industries expressing growing dissatisfaction with the job readiness of university graduates. To comprehend this complex scenario, one must consider the socio-economic backdrop of the 21st century, along with contemporary societal and corporate dynamics.

Learning Landscape

- Transformation of Universities: Originally established as knowledge and research hubs, universities now face a paradigm shift. In an era where information is freely accessible online, students often find themselves more informed than their lecturers. The urgent need for universities is to focus on skill and competency development, necessitating a radical overhaul in teaching methodologies. However, bureaucratic resistance within university administrations worldwide hinders this crucial transition.

- Job Market Shifts: The rate of job creation in traditional sectors and government roles is failing to keep pace with the number of graduates. Factors such as financial constraints, workplace automation, and increased voter scrutiny contribute to government shrinkage. While private sector employment previously thrived in manufacturing, mining, construction, and transportation, these sectors are now reducing staff due to automation and mechanisation. Conversely, the digital and technological sectors are booming, but a significant gap exists between university curricula and the skills demanded for Industry 4.0 roles.

- Curricular Obsolescence: Higher education institutions are limited by existing curricula and available teaching staff, which increasingly lag behind the rapidly evolving requirements of Industry 4.0. This mismatch widens the gap between industry expectations and academic output.

- Emergence of Practising Sciences in Industry 4.0: Unlike previous eras, Industry 4.0 is characterised by a surge in practising sciences, such as data science, cloud computing, and artificial intelligence. These fields necessitate industry-driven curricula and project-based learning, a shift from traditional classroom teaching. This change also requires instructors with industry experience and recognised certifications, adopting a coaching rather than lecturing style – a shift that many educational institutions are yet to embrace.

- Disillusionment Among Learners: Students increasingly grapple with the realisation that expensive, multi-year college degrees do not guarantee employment. This disillusionment is compounded by the fact that their most educated role models, typically lecturers with advanced degrees, often did not aspire to these teaching positions themselves.

- Rise of Vocational Training and Micro-Credentials: Learners are recognising that short vocational courses offering industry-recognised micro-credentials can be as lucrative, if not more so, than traditional college degrees. Many sought-after Industry 4.0 roles, like digital marketing or essential cloud computing skills, do not require extensive college education.

- Global Awareness and Restlessness: The internet and social media have heightened students' awareness of global educational standards and practices, leading to growing impatience with the slow pace of change in higher education. In an era where instant gratification is the norm, the sluggish adaptation of higher education institutions is a source of frustration for many learners.

Career

The career landscape for a fresh graduate in today's world is a tumultuous and unpredictable battleground, heavily influenced by a myriad of critical factors such as the graduate's field of study, geographic location, and unique blend of skills and experiences. Here's an intensified glimpse into the current realities and trends impacting recent graduates in today's fierce job market:

- COVID-19 Tsunami: The COVID-19 pandemic has unleashed a seismic shock across the job market. While industries like healthcare, technology, and e-commerce have stood resilient, sectors such as hospitality and tourism have been battered. Graduates must navigate these turbulent economic waters and assess the job market's volatile tides.

- Digital Mastery: In a world that's rapidly digitising, graduates armed with advanced digital skills – think coding wizards, data analysis gurus, and digital marketing mavens – stand at a formidable advantage. Basic digital literacy is no longer a perk; it's a battlefield necessity.

- Remote Work Revolution: Propelled by the pandemic, the shift to remote work has transformed into a full-blown revolution. Opportunities for remote or hybrid work settings are abundant, offering graduates a new realm of flexibility and challenge.

- Internship Frontlines: Those graduates who've battled in the trenches of internships or relevant work experiences carry a significant strategic advantage. These battlefields provide not just practical skills but also invaluable networks of allies.

- Networking Warfare: Building a robust professional network is akin to amassing an army. Platforms like LinkedIn are crucial arsenals for connecting with potential employers and industry veterans.

- Soft Skills Arsenal: In this intense combat zone, employers are scouting for individuals equipped with soft skills – exceptional communicators, ingenious problem-solvers, adaptable strategists, and collaborative team players.

- Continual Education Offensive: With the job market evolving at breakneck speed, a commitment to ongoing learning – further education, online courses, certifications – is a critical strategy for staying combat-ready.

- Diverse Battlegrounds: The job market presents a diverse array of battlefields – from healthcare and technology to finance, education, and the arts – each offering unique challenges and victories.

- Entrepreneurial Vanguard: For some, the path of entrepreneurship or freelance warfare beckons, offering a realm of independence and creative dominion, albeit peppered with risks and uncertainties.

- Geographic Strategy: The job terrain varies wildly by location. Certain cities and regions present more prosperous opportunities, and relocating might be a strategic move in one's career campaign.

- Career Development Fortresses: Universities and colleges often offer career development centres – fortresses providing vital resources like job search strategies, resume artillery, interview training, and networking tactics.

- Industry Reconnaissance: Conducting deep reconnaissance into one's chosen field – through industry publications, professional organisations, and networking events – is crucial for understanding the unique challenges and trends of the field.

Remember, the job market is a dynamic and ever-changing battlefield. Staying adaptable, seizing a diverse range of opportunities, and seeking the wisdom of experienced mentors can be invaluable strategies for fresh graduates navigating this complex and competitive arena.

Timing

In-depth exploration of the monumental impact of timing on career success reveals that its significance often eclipses other factors like team quality, execution strategy, or funding. This truth resonates both in the corporate world and individual career trajectories. Here's an expanded and intense look at the critical dimensions of timing in a career:

- Intersection of Opportunity, Luck, and Timing: The serendipitous convergence of being in the opportune place at the perfect moment can catapult a career to new heights. Imagine landing a pivotal job offer or being present during a major industry upheaval – these are not mere chances but career-defining moments born from the nexus of timing, opportunity, and luck.

- The Role of Political Stability and Global Economics: In an era that is historically peaceful and economically flourishing, even with occasional conflicts, the broad acceptance of capitalism, even in traditionally communist nations like China, creates a fertile ground for career growth. Understanding how global political dynamics foster trade can be a game-changer for strategic career planning.

- Navigating Economic and Industry Cycles: Profound insights into the rhythmic patterns of industries – their growth, stability, and decline – can be career game-changers. For example, entering a burgeoning sector could mean better opportunities and increased financial rewards.

- Strategic Personal Development Timing: The right timing in pursuing education, acquiring new skills, and personal growth can dramatically elevate your marketability and competitiveness. It's about syncing your personal development clock with the market's pulse.

- Harmonising with Market Demands: Aligning one's career with the ever-shifting market demand for specific skills or services can lead to unmatched job security and potentially lucrative earnings. It's about riding the wave of market needs.

- Optimal Timing of Career Transitions: The decision to switch jobs, industries, or roles, and its timing, can be a make-or-break factor in a career. A well-timed leap can open doors to uncharted opportunities, whereas a mistimed one could lead to professional setbacks.

- Networking and Relationships in Time's Web: The chronology of forging key professional relationships – meeting mentors, collaborators, or influential contacts – can significantly shape your career path. It's about connecting the dots of relationships over time.

- Technological Evolution and Timing: As technology disrupts and reshapes industries, being adept and timely in embracing these changes can set you apart in your field. It's about being a timely adopter and innovator.

- Life Stages and Career Choices: Different life stages call for different career decisions. The timing of starting a family, pursuing further education, or taking risks – all these impact your career's trajectory in profound ways.

- Alignment with Personal Goals and Values: The synchronisation of career moves with personal aspirations, values, and goals is crucial. Making career decisions that resonate with your inner compass at the right time can lead to not just professional success but profound personal fulfilment.

- Adaptability Timed to Perfection: In a world where change is the only constant, the ability to adapt – and to time this adaptability – can be a decisive career advantage. It's about staying agile and responsive to the ever-evolving job landscape.

In essence, timing in a career is not just about serendipity; it's a complex amalgamation of strategic planning, intuitive decision-making, and adapting to evolving circumstances. It's about finding that sweet spot where preparation meets opportunity, leading to a harmonious and successful professional journey.

Navigating Industry 4.0 and Beyond: Unleashing Career Opportunities in Industry 5.0

"In the transition from Industry 4.0 to 5.0, the fusion of technology and human ingenuity redefines success, placing skills, attitude, and continuous learning at the forefront of career growth."

The advent of Industry 4.0 marked a transformative era in the global job market, characterised by the integration of digital technologies, automation, and data-driven decision-making processes. As we stand on the cusp of Industry 5.0, the landscape is evolving even further, creating unprecedented opportunities for job seekers. Let us explore how individuals can harness the changing dynamics of Industry 4.0 and seamlessly transition into the promising realms of Industry 5.0, where skills, attitude, and mindset often outweigh traditional qualifications.

The Rise of Industry 4.0

Industry 4.0 brought about a paradigm shift in the way businesses operate. Automation, artificial intelligence (AI), the Internet of

Things (IoT), and big data became integral components of industrial processes, optimising efficiency and productivity. Traditional job roles underwent a metamorphosis, with a growing emphasis on technology-driven skills. As a result, industries started seeking talent with a versatile skill set that extended beyond academic qualifications.

Skills Over Qualifications

In Industry 4.0, employers began recognising the limitations of traditional qualifications in meeting the dynamic demands of rapidly evolving sectors. This shift was particularly evident in tech-driven industries like IT, cybersecurity, and data science. Employers sought candidates who possessed hands-on experience, practical skills, and a proactive attitude towards learning. Certifications and micro-credentials gained prominence, allowing job seekers to acquire targeted skills relevant to specific roles.

Evolving Industries: Breaking the Mould

The transition from Industry 4.0 to Industry 5.0 is marked by even more agility and adaptability in industries. Sectors such as renewable energy, biotechnology, and sustainable development are emerging as powerhouses, and they are characterised by a departure from rigid qualification requirements. These industries are less concerned with degrees and more focused on the tangible skills and innovative thinking that candidates bring to the table.

Rapid Career Growth in Newer Sectors

The evolving nature of Industry 5.0 creates an environment where career growth is not bound by traditional hierarchies. Startups and innovative companies within these newer sectors are often more open to promoting talent based on merit rather than years of experience. This offers job seekers the chance to climb the career ladder swiftly, provided they can demonstrate their value through practical contributions and a forward-thinking mindset.

Disproportionate Income Opportunities

One of the most appealing aspects of Industry 5.0 is the potential for disproportionate income opportunities compared to traditional roles. The rapid growth and demand for specialised skills create a scenario where skilled individuals can negotiate competitive salaries. In contrast to traditional industries, where income is often linked to years of experience, Industry 5.0 rewards individuals who can contribute significantly to innovation and problem-solving.

The Role of Soft Skills and Mindset

As industries transition to Industry 5.0, soft skills and the right mindset become crucial differentiators. Communication, adaptability, creativity, and critical thinking are highly valued in dynamic environments. Employers recognise that a candidate with a growth mindset and the ability to navigate ambiguity can contribute significantly to the organisation's success. Job seekers should invest in developing these soft skills to complement their technical expertise.

Embracing Continuous Learning

Industry 5.0 is synonymous with constant innovation and evolution. Job seekers looking to harness the opportunities within this realm must adopt a mindset of continuous learning. Staying updated with the latest industry trends, acquiring new skills, and being open to ongoing professional development are key factors in staying relevant and competitive.

Networking and Collaboration

In Industry 5.0, success is often a result of collaboration and networking. The interconnectedness of industries and the emphasis on cross-disciplinary approaches require individuals to build a robust professional network. Networking not only opens doors to new opportunities but also facilitates knowledge exchange and collaborative problem-solving. Job seekers should actively participate in industry events, online forums, and professional associations to expand their network.

Leveraging Technology for Job Search

In the age of Industry 5.0, the traditional job search methods are no longer sufficient. Job seekers need to leverage technology to showcase their skills and connect with potential employers. Building an online presence through professional networking platforms, creating a digital portfolio, and utilising AI-driven job matching tools are essential strategies for staying visible in the competitive job market.

Embracing Diversity and Inclusion

Industry 5.0 places a strong emphasis on diversity and inclusion. Companies recognise the value of a diverse workforce in fostering innovation and creativity. Job seekers should actively seek out employers who prioritise diversity and inclusion, as these organisations are more likely to provide an inclusive and supportive environment for career growth.

The transition from Industry 4.0 to Industry 5.0 presents a myriad of opportunities for job seekers willing to adapt and embrace change. The evolving industries in Industry 5.0 are less rigid in their qualification requirements, focusing more on skills, attitude, and mindset. Rapid career growth and disproportionate income opportunities await those who can navigate this dynamic landscape, making it essential for job seekers to invest in continuous learning, soft skills development, and strategic networking. As Industry 5.0 unfolds, it is not just a career evolution; it is a revolution in how we perceive and approach work in the 21st century.

The Dynamic Landscape of Future Professions

"The future of work will be defined not by the color of one's collar but by the seamless blend of human expertise and technological innovation."

The current nature of the global workforce is confusing for a layperson. The distinctions between blue collar and white-collar jobs are becoming increasingly blurred. The future of work is characterised by a fusion of technology, innovation, and a profound shift in societal values. As we navigate this uncharted terrain, the demand for specific skills is reshaping the job market, ushering in a new era where both traditional and emerging professions will coexist in harmony.

- *Blue Collar Renaissance: A Resurgence of Vital Professions*

  Contrary to the apprehensions surrounding the automation apocalypse, blue collar jobs are poised for a renaissance. Occupations that were once overshadowed by the allure of technology are now emerging as indispensable pillars of our society.

- *Transportation Revolution: The Enduring Demand for Truck Drivers*

  In an era dominated by self-driving vehicles and drones, the role of truck drivers remains irreplaceable. The complex, dynamic nature of road navigation demands human intuition, adaptability, and decision-making capabilities that artificial intelligence struggles to replicate. As the backbone of supply chains, truck drivers not only transport goods but also ensure the seamless functioning of the global economy.

  Moreover, the growing demand for just-in-time logistics and the expansion of e-commerce has elevated the significance of truck drivers to unprecedented levels. With an acute shortage of skilled drivers, the wages for this profession are expected to surge, offering an enticing prospect for those who choose to navigate the open road.

- *Cultivating Tomorrow's Harvest: Agricultural Machine Operators*

  As agriculture undergoes a digital transformation, the role of agricultural machine operators is evolving into a technologically sophisticated profession. The integration of drones, precision agriculture, and autonomous machinery requires skilled individuals to operate, troubleshoot, and optimise these systems. While technology streamlines processes, the need for human oversight remains paramount to ensure sustainable and efficient food production.

  The agricultural sector is experiencing a paradigm shift where individuals with a deep understanding of both traditional farming practices and cutting-edge technology are in high demand. As climate change heightens the importance of resilient and adaptive agricultural practices, the role of these operators becomes not only critical but also economically rewarding.

- *Powering the Future: Alternate Energy Installers*

In the quest for sustainable energy solutions, the demand for alternate energy installers is skyrocketing. Whether it's solar panels, wind turbines, or other renewable sources, the installation and maintenance of these systems require a skilled workforce. Blue collar professionals trained in electrical work, engineering, and environmental sciences are at the forefront of building a cleaner, greener future.

Governments and corporations worldwide are investing heavily in renewable energy, creating a surge in job opportunities for those who choose to harness the power of the wind and the sun. As the world pivots towards eco-friendly alternatives, alternate energy installers are not only meeting the demand for sustainable solutions but also benefiting from a job market hungry for their expertise.

- *The Plumbing Renaissance: Masters of the Fluid World*

In the heart of every modern infrastructure, the role of plumbers is indispensable. As smart homes and cities become the norm, the complexity of plumbing systems is increasing exponentially. From integrating IoT devices to ensuring water efficiency, plumbers are not only fixing leaks but are also the guardians of a sustainable and connected water infrastructure.

The resurgence of this age-old trade is characterised by a blend of traditional craftsmanship and contemporary technological expertise. Plumbers of the future will not only possess the skills to fix conventional issues but also the technical know-how to navigate the intricacies of smart plumbing systems, making them an integral part of the evolving urban landscape.

White-Collar Metamorphosis: Technology as the Cornerstone

In tandem with the revival of blue collar professions, the white-collar sector is undergoing a metamorphosis fuelled by technology and the need for human-centred expertise. While automation and artificial intelligence continue to reshape industries, certain professions are becoming increasingly reliant on human judgement, empathy, and nuanced decision-making.

- *Healing Hands: The Unmatched Value of Healthcare Professionals*

  The healthcare sector stands at the forefront of the white-collar job revolution. As technology advances, healthcare professionals are leveraging innovative tools for diagnostics, treatment, and patient care. However, the essence of healthcare lies in the human touch – the ability to empathise, communicate, and make nuanced decisions based on a patient's unique circumstances.

  Doctors, nurses, and other healthcare professionals are not merely recipients of technological advancements; they are the architects of a healthcare system where compassion and expertise harmoniously coexist with cutting-edge technology. In this era of personalised medicine, healthcare professionals are at the nexus of human wellbeing and technological innovation.

- *Guardians of Four-Legged Friends: Veterinarians in the Digital Age*

  As companionship with animals continues to be an integral part of human life, the role of veterinarians is evolving to encompass a myriad of challenges. From advanced diagnostics to telehealth consultations, veterinarians are leveraging technology to provide comprehensive care to our four-legged friends. Yet, the essence of veterinary medicine remains deeply rooted in the ability to understand and respond to the non-verbal cues of animals.

As the world acknowledges the significance of the human-animal bond, veterinarians find themselves at the intersection of technological advancement and compassionate care. The demand for skilled professionals who can navigate this delicate balance is soaring, making veterinary medicine a sought-after and rewarding career.

- *Beyond Tooth and Gum: Dentistry in the Age of Innovation*

Dentistry, often-overlooked in conversations about future professions, is undergoing a profound transformation. From 3D printing of dental prosthetics to virtual consultations and advanced imaging technologies, dentists are embracing innovation to provide more efficient and patient-centric care. However, the crux of dentistry lies in the meticulous expertise of human hands, and the ability to tailor treatment plans to individual patient needs.

As oral health gains recognition as a vital component of overall wellbeing, the demand for dentists who can seamlessly integrate technology into their practice while upholding the personalised aspect of care is escalating. Dentistry is not just about teeth; it's about crafting smiles and ensuring the overall health and confidence of individuals.

- *Minds Matter: Mental Health Professionals in the Digital Frontier*

The increasing recognition of mental health as an integral aspect of overall wellbeing has catapulted mental health professionals into the forefront of the white-collar job market. Technology has played a dual role in this transformation, both as a tool for diagnosis and treatment and as a facilitator for breaking down barriers to mental health care.

Psychologists, counsellors, and therapists are not only adapting to virtual platforms but are also leveraging technology to enhance the effectiveness of interventions. However, the essence of mental health care lies in the ability to establish a genuine human connection, to empathise, and to guide individuals on their journey to wellbeing. In the era of digital connections, mental health professionals are the guardians of our collective mental resilience.

- *Navigating Financial Horizons: The Human Touch in Personal Finance*

In a world increasingly driven by algorithms and robo-advisers, the role of human financial experts becomes all the more pivotal. While technology can provide data-driven insights and automate certain financial processes, the nuances of personal finance require a human touch. Financial advisers, planners, and analysts play a crucial role in translating complex financial data into actionable plans tailored to individual goals and aspirations.

The advent of fintech has not replaced but rather augmented the importance of human expertise in personal finance. The ability to understand the unique financial circumstances of individuals, provide personalised advice, and navigate the ever-evolving landscape of financial instruments ensures that the demand for skilled professionals in this sector remains robust.

- *Crafting Identities: Personal Branding in the Digital Age*

In an era where personal and professional lives seamlessly converge on digital platforms, the concept of personal branding has gained unprecedented importance. Individuals, entrepreneurs, and professionals alike are recognising the need to curate and communicate a compelling personal brand. In this landscape, experts in personal branding have emerged as invaluable guides, helping individuals navigate the intricacies of online presence and reputation management.

The fusion of psychology, marketing, and digital literacy is at the core of personal branding. Professionals in this field are not just social media strategists but architects of online personas, understanding the delicate balance between authenticity and strategic communication. As the digital footprint of individuals becomes increasingly influential, the demand for personal branding experts is set to soar.

- *The Sky's the Limit: Pilots in the Era of Smart Aviation*

Amidst the proliferation of autonomous technologies, the role of pilots remains unparalleled in ensuring the safety and efficiency of air travel. While autopilot systems and advanced navigation technologies have become integral components of modern aircraft, the human touch in the cockpit is irreplaceable. Pilots are not merely operators but decision-makers who navigate through complex scenarios, unforeseen challenges, and dynamic weather conditions.

Smart aviation is not about replacing pilots with machines but enhancing their capabilities through innovative technologies. As the aviation industry continues to grow, so does the demand for skilled pilots who can seamlessly integrate technological advancements into their decision-making processes. Pilots of the future are not just aviators; they are stewards of safe and efficient air travel in the digital age.

- *Bridging the Divide: A Confluence of Blue and White-Collar Expertise*

The future of work is not a binary choice between blue collar and white-collar professions; rather, it is a tapestry woven with the threads of human expertise and technological innovation. The key to success in this dynamic landscape lies in the ability to bridge the gap between the traditional and the futuristic, to seamlessly integrate human judgement with technological prowess.

As the world hurtles towards an era where the boundaries between man and machine blur, the demand for skills that define our humanity becomes more pronounced. The ability to empathise, communicate effectively, make nuanced decisions, and adapt to evolving circumstances are the true currencies of the future job market.

The professions of tomorrow will be defined not by the colour of the collar but by the depth of expertise and the ability to navigate the intricate dance between humanity and technology. Whether you find yourself on the open road, tending to the wellbeing of animals, crafting financial strategies, or soaring through the skies, the future is a mosaic where every skill, whether blue or white-collar, has a vital role to play in shaping the world we inhabit.

Essential Skills for Industry 4.0

"Embracing the convergence of digital, physical, and biological realms, Industry 4.0 challenges fresh graduates to master a blend of technical and soft skills, forging a path to innovation and resilience in an ever-evolving landscape."

In an age where the lines between the physical, digital, and biological spheres are increasingly blurred, Industry 4.0 stands as a beacon of transformative change. This new industrial revolution, marked by the advent of digital technologies, automation, artificial intelligence (AI), and data-driven decision-making, is reshaping the very fabric of business and manufacturing landscapes. For fresh graduates stepping into this dynamic environment, the onus is on acquiring a robust skill set that aligns with the demands of this era. This chapter delves into the essential skills—both technical and soft—that are indispensable for fresh graduates to excel in the realm of Industry 4.0, supplemented by real-life workplace examples to illustrate their importance.

Technical Skills

Digital Literacy

Digital literacy serves as the cornerstone of navigating Industry 4.0. It encompasses proficiency in using software, mobile applications, and online platforms for accessing, analysing, and sharing information. A real-life example is the use of Microsoft Office or Google Workspace for collaborative projects, where understanding these platforms' nuances can significantly enhance productivity and efficiency in the workplace.

Data Analytics and Data Science

The capacity to gather, analyse, and derive insights from data stands as a critical skill. Fresh graduates should be conversant with data analytics tools, visualisation techniques, and statistical analysis. For instance, a marketing analyst leveraging Python to sift through customer data, identifying trends that inform targeted marketing strategies, exemplifies the practical application of these skills.

Machine Learning and Artificial Intelligence

Understanding AI and machine learning fundamentals is becoming increasingly crucial. A practical example is a software developer employing machine learning algorithms to improve user experience on a retail website, making personalised product recommendations based on browsing history.

Programming and Coding Skills

Programming languages like Python, Java, or JavaScript are invaluable, enabling graduates to contribute to software development, automation, and digital projects. For example, a graduate developing a mobile application that simplifies online transactions for users demonstrates the practical utility of coding skills.

Cybersecurity

With the digitalisation of assets, knowledge of cybersecurity best practices is paramount to protect sensitive information. An example includes IT professionals implementing encryption and firewall strategies to secure company data against cyber threats.

IoT (Internet of Things)

Understanding IoT and its applications, such as designing smart home systems that automate lighting, heating, and security, showcases the relevance of IoT skills in improving efficiency and quality of life.

Cloud Computing

Knowledge of cloud services (AWS, Azure, Google Cloud) for data storage and application deployment is fundamental. Using cloud platforms to facilitate remote work environments, where team members can access project files from anywhere, illustrates cloud computing's impact.

Blockchain

Blockchain's understanding, while niche, can be a significant advantage in sectors like finance and supply chain, exemplified by the development of secure, transparent transaction systems.

Robotics and Automation

Knowledge of robotics and automation is key, as seen in manufacturing, where automated assembly lines increase production rates and decrease human error.

3D Printing

3D printing technology is revolutionising fields such as healthcare, where custom prosthetics can be designed and produced to meet individual patient needs, showcasing the technology's practical applications.

Soft Skills

Adaptability

The rapid pace of technological change necessitates adaptability and a willingness to learn. A software engineer learning new programming languages to stay relevant in the job market exemplifies this skill.

Problem-Solving

Analysing complex problems and developing innovative solutions are crucial. Engineers troubleshooting production line issues by devising efficient and cost-effective solutions highlight the importance of problem-solving skills.

Effective Communication

The ability to convey complex technical concepts to non-technical stakeholders is vital, such as a project manager explaining the benefits of a new software tool to company executives.

Collaboration

The trend towards cross-functional teams demands excellent collaboration skills, seen in diverse project teams where members bring different expertise to solve a problem collectively.

Leadership

Leadership, even at entry levels, involves leading projects and inspiring others. A team lead coordinating a group project, ensuring deadlines are met while fostering a positive team environment, illustrates leadership in action.

Time Management

Effective time management is essential in a fast-paced environment, such as a developer juggling multiple coding tasks and meeting tight deadlines without compromising quality.

Resilience

The capacity to bounce back from setbacks is key, exemplified by entrepreneurs who face initial failures but persevere to eventually succeed in their ventures.

Ethical Decision-Making

Ethical considerations in technology use are becoming more critical. A data scientist ensuring that AI models do not propagate bias represents the importance of ethical decision-making.

Customer Focus

Understanding customer needs and delivering solutions that meet their expectations is crucial, as seen in user experience designers creating intuitive apps based on user feedback.

Networking

Building a professional network is vital for career growth. Active participation in industry conferences and online forums can open doors to job opportunities and collaborations.

Interdisciplinary Knowledge

Business Acumen

Knowledge of business operations, market analysis, and financial management is crucial, as demonstrated by entrepreneurs who successfully launch startups by understanding both the market and the technology.

Industry-Specific Knowledge

Industry-specific insights, such as regulatory compliance in the pharmaceutical sector, ensure that graduates can navigate the nuances of their chosen fields effectively.

Environmental Sustainability

With increasing focus on sustainability, understanding environmental impacts and sustainable practices is essential, exemplified by companies integrating green technologies into their operations.

The Fourth Industrial Revolution demands a comprehensive skill set from fresh graduates, encompassing technical prowess in areas like digital literacy, data analytics, and cybersecurity, as well as soft skills such as adaptability, communication, and leadership. Furthermore, an understanding of business dynamics, industry specifics, and sustainability issues can provide a competitive edge. Equipping themselves with these skills, fresh graduates are poised to navigate the complexities of Industry 4.0, contributing to the ongoing transformation and advancement of industries worldwide. The journey from academia to the dynamic world of Industry 4.0 is both challenging and rewarding, offering endless opportunities for those prepared to embrace the future.

The Dawn of Industry 5.0: Embracing Humanity's Next Leap Forward

"Industry 5.0 redefines progress by merging human creativity with technological precision, fostering a future where innovation is both human-centered and ethically grounded."

As we stand on the cusp of Industry 5.0, we find ourselves at a pivotal moment in human history. Building upon the digital backbone of Industry 4.0, this next phase in industrial evolution promises to reintegrate the human element into the technological tapestry, marking a shift towards a more symbiotic relationship between humans and machines. This chapter delves into the essence of Industry 5.0, its implications for humanity, and the strategies individuals can employ to thrive in this new era.

The Essence of Industry 5.0

Industry 4.0 laid the groundwork with its focus on automation, artificial intelligence (AI), the Internet of Things (IoT), and smart factories. In contrast, Industry 5.0 represents a paradigm shift towards a human-centric approach. It envisions a world where technology augments human capabilities, rather than replacing them, emphasising creativity, empathy, and personal touch alongside technological efficiency.

The core of Industry 5.0 lies in the synergy between humans and machines. Advanced robotics and AI systems are seen not as replacements but as partners that can take on physically demanding or repetitive tasks, allowing humans to focus on areas that require cognitive, creative, and emotional intelligence. This collaboration aims to enhance productivity, foster innovation, and ensure that the benefits of technology are more equitably distributed across society.

Human-Centric Manufacturing and Production

At the heart of Industry 5.0 is the concept of human-centric manufacturing. This approach prioritises the wellbeing and creativity of workers, ensuring that technology serves to enhance the quality of life rather than diminish the value of human labour. It involves designing work environments where machines handle hazardous or tedious tasks, enabling humans to engage in more meaningful and creative work.

Mass personalisation is a key feature of this era, blending the efficiency of mass production with the individuality of customisation. Through the use of AI and data analytics, businesses can create products and experiences uniquely tailored to each consumer's preferences, fostering a deeper connection between companies and their customers.

Preparing for Success in Industry 5.0

Thriving in the era of Industry 5.0 requires a proactive approach to personal and professional development. Here are strategies individuals can adopt to set themselves up for success:

Lifelong Learning: The rapid pace of technological advancement necessitates a commitment to continuous education. Embrace the learning opportunities presented by online courses, workshops, and seminars to stay abreast of the latest technologies and methodologies.

Cultivate Creativity and Emotional Intelligence: In an era where machines excel at routine tasks, human creativity, empathy, and interpersonal skills become invaluable assets. Cultivating these abilities can set individuals apart in the job market.

Adaptability and Flexibility: The ability to adapt to new technologies and workflows is crucial. Being open to change and willing to pivot when necessary will be key traits for professionals navigating the shifting landscapes of Industry 5.0.

Collaboration Skills: As human-machine collaboration becomes more prevalent, the ability to work effectively alongside AI systems and robots will be essential. Understanding the strengths and limitations of these technologies will enable more effective teamwork.

Ethical Considerations and Sustainability: With great power comes great responsibility. As technology continues to evolve, ethical considerations, particularly regarding data privacy and environmental sustainability, will take centre stage. Professionals who can navigate these complex issues while driving innovation will be highly sought-after.

Industry 5.0 heralds a future where technology and humanity converge in ways previously unimaginable, creating opportunities for enhanced creativity, productivity, and personal fulfilment. By emphasising the unique contributions of human creativity and emotional intelligence, this new era promises not only to advance our technological capabilities but also to foster a more inclusive and sustainable future.

As we embark on this journey, the key to success lies in our ability to leverage the strengths of both humans and machines, embracing the opportunities for growth and innovation that lie ahead. By preparing ourselves with the right skills, mindset, and ethical considerations, we can all play a part in shaping a future where technology amplifies our human potential, creating a world that benefits all of humanity.

Part 2

SKILLS FOR FUTURE CAREERS

"Adaptability and continuous learning are the cornerstone skills for future careers, as technology and global dynamics reshape the job market at an unprecedented pace."

The Halo Effect – Acquiring Divine Leadership Skills

"Role models need to be emulated not just idolized."

Throughout history, gods and great leaders have often been surrounded by an aura, a symbolic halo that signifies their divine or extraordinary qualities. This halo effect is not limited to religious or mythological figures; it can also be observed in the realm of modern leadership. In this chapter, we will explore the concept of the halo effect and how you can acquire similar qualities in your life through specific actions and skills development.

The Halo Effect Explained

The halo effect is a cognitive bias that occurs when we perceive someone as being inherently good, capable, or trustworthy based on one or a few positive attributes or actions. It's a phenomenon that has been observed in our perception of gods, revered historical figures, and contemporary leaders alike. People like Mahatma Gandhi, Nelson Mandela, Martin Luther King Jr., and even Steve

Jobs are all examples of individuals who have been regarded with a certain halo effect.

The Five Halo Skills

1. *Great Mindset*

Developing a great mindset is the foundation of acquiring the halo effect. It involves the ability to confront your fears and channel them toward personal and professional growth. Think of historical figures like Winston Churchill, who faced immense challenges during World War II but maintained an unwavering belief in victory. By cultivating a mindset that embraces challenges and adapts to change, you can tap into the optimal velocity for success in your life.

2. *Indistractability*

In today's world, distractions abound. To acquire the halo effect, you must master the skill of indistractability. This means being able to focus for extended periods without succumbing to the constant demands on your attention. Leaders like Elon Musk, who can immerse themselves in complex projects without getting derailed by external noise, are exemplars of this skill.

3. *Conversationality and Influenceability*

To become a divine leader, you must be able to communicate effectively and hold an audience's attention. Your ability to influence individuals or groups through your words, actions, and deeds is a crucial aspect of the halo effect. Look at figures like Maya Angelou, whose poetry and speeches inspired generations.

By honing your conversational and influencing skills, you can resonate with others on a deeper level and lead with impact.

4. Role Modelling and Self-Management

Leaders who inspire trust and admiration often practise balance and restraint in their daily lives. They serve as role models by exhibiting consistency in their behaviour and decision-making. Think of leaders like Mother Teresa, who dedicated her life to helping others while maintaining unwavering moral principles. By consistently demonstrating self-management and serving as a positive example, you can foster trust and followership.

5. Credibility and Personal Branding

Lastly, one can only be a leader if they have followers. To attract followers, you need a personal brand founded on credibility. Look at figures like Nelson Mandela, who spent decades in prison but emerged as a symbol of moral authority and reconciliation. Building a strong personal brand rooted in integrity and authenticity is essential for acquiring the halo effect.

Cultivating Your Halo

Acquiring the halo effect is not a mystical process reserved for gods and mythical figures. It is a set of skills and qualities that can be developed through conscious effort and practice. By embracing a great mindset, mastering indistractability, honing your conversational and influencing skills, exemplifying role modelling and self-management, and building a credible personal brand, you can cultivate your own halo effect.

In the following chapters, we will delve deeper into each of these halo skills, providing you with practical exercises, real-life examples, and actionable advice to help you develop these qualities and become a divine leader in your own right. Remember, the halo effect is not reserved for the chosen few; it can be acquired by those who are willing to invest in their personal and professional growth. Simply having these skills is not enough. These skills need to be practiced and displayed in the pursuit of some purpose that is fuelled by passion and ultimately results in visible success for themselves and society at large. Now, let us look at the five "Halo Skills" in greater detail.

The Power of a Great Mindset

"A great mindset converts fear into fuel for growth & success."

In a world where automation and artificial intelligence are rapidly reshaping the employment landscape, the invaluable skill of developing a great mindset has never been more critical. Beyond the well-known concept of a growth mindset, there exists another dimension of mental strength that is equally vital in the pursuit of professional and personal success — the Great Mindset.

The Great Mindset goes beyond the notion of embracing challenges and learning from failures, as emphasised by a growth mindset. It encompasses the ability to confront one's deepest fears and anxieties and transform them into powerful catalysts for growth. It's about harnessing the fear of the unknown and leveraging it to propel oneself forward with optimal velocity.

The Great Mindset Unveiled

Imagine a young woman named Sarah, who was once paralysed by her fear of public speaking. She avoided any opportunity that required her to address an audience, limiting her career growth and personal development. But one day, she decided to confront her fear head-on.

Sarah didn't just seek to improve her public speaking skills; she sought to understand the root of her fear and how it was holding her back. She began attending workshops, working with a coach, and gradually pushing herself to speak in front of small groups of friends. With time and relentless effort, she not only conquered her fear but also discovered a passion for motivational speaking.

Sarah's transformation is a prime example of the Great Mindset in action. Instead of letting her fear hold her back, she channelled it into an incredible source of motivation and growth. She not only overcame her limitations but also found a new career path that brought her immense satisfaction and success.

The Great Mindset in the Workplace

In the professional realm, the Great Mindset is a game-changer. Consider John, a mid-level manager in a tech company, who was facing a looming company-wide restructuring. His initial reaction was fear and anxiety about potential layoffs and changes in his role. But instead of succumbing to these negative emotions, John decided to embrace them.

John dove into the restructuring process, proactively seeking opportunities to contribute to the company's transformation. He volunteered to lead a team tasked with implementing innovative changes in their department, leveraging his fear as a driving force to excel.

As a result, John not only secured his position but also gained recognition for his leadership during a challenging period.

His Great Mindset propelled him to navigate uncertainty with confidence and emerge as a valuable asset to the organisation.

Cultivating a Great Mindset

- Developing a Great Mindset is not an overnight process; it requires patience, self-awareness, and dedication. Here are some key steps to help you cultivate this invaluable skill:

- Self-Reflection: Take time to understand your fears and anxieties. Identify their roots and how they may be holding you back.

- Seek Guidance: Don't be afraid to seek guidance from mentors, coaches, or therapists who can help you work through your fears and anxieties.

- Challenge Yourself: Gradually expose yourself to situations that trigger your fears. Start small and work your way up.

- Embrace Failure: Understand that setbacks and failures are part of the journey. Learn from them and use them as stepping stones to success.

- Stay Resilient: Cultivate resilience by developing a positive outlook and maintaining a strong support system.

In the ever-evolving job market of the future, the ability to develop a Great Mindset will set you apart from the competition. It's not just about embracing growth; it's about using your fears as a powerful force for transformation and personal evolution. As you journey towards developing a Great Mindset, you'll find yourself not only conquering your fears but also achieving unparalleled professional and personal success.

The Indistractable Advantage

"Indistractability is not just a skill, it is a superpower. "

In the bustling city of New York, a young woman named Sarah sat at her desk in a co-working space, fully engrossed in her work. The office buzzed with activity as people chatted, typed, and took phone calls, but Sarah remained undistracted. She had mastered the invaluable skill of indistractability in a world filled with constant digital noise.

Sarah's story is just one example of how mastering indistractability can open doors to future job opportunities and career success in our cluttered times. In this chapter, we will explore real-life examples of individuals who have harnessed the power of focus and discipline to thrive in the age of social media and endless distractions.

The Rise of Indistractability

Before diving into our real-life examples, let's take a moment to understand why indistractability is such a crucial skill in today's world. The digital age has brought with it an unprecedented amount of information and connectivity. While these advancements have revolutionised the way we work and live, they have also created an environment where our attention is constantly under siege.

In a world where social media notifications, emails, and endless streams of content are constantly competing for our attention, the ability to focus and stay indistractable has become an invaluable skill for the future workforce.

Social media platforms, email notifications, messaging apps, and streaming services all compete for our attention, making it increasingly difficult to stay focused on tasks that require deep work and critical thinking. The ability to resist these distractions and concentrate on what truly matters has become a valuable skill set for the future job market.

The Cost of Distraction

Before delving into the strategies to become indistractable, it's essential to understand the profound impact that distraction can have on our lives and careers. Distraction not only hinders productivity but also affects our overall wellbeing. The constant interruption of our work by pings and notifications can lead to stress, decreased job satisfaction, and even burnout.

Moreover, the attention economy, fuelled by social media platforms and advertising, seeks to capture our focus for their profit. The more distracted we are, the more these companies benefit. It's crucial to recognise that our attention is a limited and valuable resource, and guarding it against constant distractions is of paramount importance.

Sarah's Story: Mastering Indistractability

Sarah, the young woman in the co-working space, had learned to protect her focus with unwavering discipline. She shared her experiences and insights with us, shedding light on how she had honed her indistractability.

Sarah worked as a freelance graphic designer. In the early stages of her career, she struggled with distractions and often found herself falling behind on deadlines. It wasn't until she realised that her inability to stay focused was holding her back that she decided to act.

She implemented several strategies to boost her indistractability:

- Time Blocking: Sarah set specific blocks of time for focused work and scheduled short breaks for checking emails and social media. During her work blocks, she turned off notifications and put her phone on silent mode.

- Digital Minimalism: Recognising that many of her distractions came from unnecessary apps and notifications, Sarah went through a digital detox. She deleted apps that didn't serve her work-related goals and turned off non-essential notifications.

- Creating a Distraction-Free Environment: Sarah invested in noise-cancelling headphones and used website blockers to prevent access to distracting websites during work hours.

- Mindfulness and Meditation: She incorporated mindfulness and meditation into her daily routine to improve her ability to focus and resist the temptation of distractions.

The result of Sarah's efforts was remarkable. She not only met her deadlines consistently but also produced higher-quality work. Her reputation as a reliable and skilled designer began to spread, and she started receiving more client referrals, leading to a flourishing freelance business.

The Business Magnate: Elon Musk

Elon Musk, the visionary CEO of SpaceX and Tesla, is another shining example of indistractability. In an age where CEOs are often overwhelmed by meetings, emails, and social commitments, Musk manages to lead two groundbreaking companies simultaneously while staying remarkably focused on his missions.

Musk's secret lies in his strict time management and prioritisation of deep work. He blocks out chunks of time for focused thinking and often resorts to sending concise emails or holding shorter meetings to conserve his attention for what truly matters: advancing humanity through sustainable transportation and space exploration.

The Creative Genius: J.K. Rowling

J.K. Rowling, the author of the beloved Harry Potter series, faced her fair share of distractions and challenges on her path to success. As a single mother living on welfare, she found herself in a chaotic and distracting environment. However, Rowling's determination to write her novel and her indistractability transformed her life.

She frequently visited cafes to escape her noisy home environment and wrote during her daughter's nap times. Her unwavering commitment to her craft, even in the face of adversity, led to the creation of one of the most successful literary franchises in history.

The Tech Entrepreneur: Tristan Harris

Tristan Harris, a former Google Design Ethicist, recognised the harmful effects of technology addiction and distractions in our society. He co-founded the Centre for Humane Technology and became a vocal advocate for designing products and services that respect users' attention.

Harris's work highlights the growing demand for individuals who can not only resist distractions but also actively work to make technology more conducive to human wellbeing. His career transition from the tech industry to advocacy underscores the importance of indistractability in shaping the future of technology.

Indistractability is not just about resisting the allure of social media or ignoring incoming emails. It's about proactively managing your attention, setting clear priorities, and staying focused on what truly matters. The indistractable worker is one who can navigate the cluttered landscape of modern life without succumbing to every shiny digital temptation.

Cultivating Indistractability

1. Define Your Values and Goals

To become indistractable, you must first define your values and long-term goals. Knowing what truly matters to you helps you prioritise your time and attention accordingly. When you have a clear sense of purpose, it becomes easier to resist distractions that do not align with your values.

2. Create a Distraction-Free Environment

Design your physical and digital workspaces to minimise potential distractions. This may involve turning off notifications, silencing your phone, or using website blockers during focused work periods. A clutter-free environment can significantly enhance your ability to stay indistractable.

3. Master the Art of Time Management

Effective time management is a critical aspect of indistractability. Techniques like the Pomodoro Technique, time blocking, and task batching can help you structure your day and allocate dedicated time for focused work. These methods encourage deep work and make it more challenging for distractions to creep in.

4. Practice Mindfulness

Mindfulness meditation can help improve your ability to stay focused. By training your mind to be present in the moment, you become better equipped to recognise and resist distractions as they arise. Regular mindfulness practice can increase your overall attention span and enhance your indistractability.

5. Set Boundaries

Establish clear boundaries with colleagues, friends, and family regarding your availability and work hours. Let them know when you are not to be disturbed unless it's an emergency. Respect for your boundaries can help reduce external distractions.

6. *Learn to Say No*

Indistractable individuals understand that they cannot say yes to every request or opportunity that comes their way. Learning to say no, politely but firmly, is essential to maintain focus on your priorities.

7. *Embrace Boredom*

In a world of constant stimulation, it may feel uncomfortable to embrace moments of boredom. However, allowing your mind to wander and daydream can be beneficial for creativity and problem-solving. It's during these moments of quiet reflection that breakthrough ideas often emerge.

Indistractability is a skill that will become increasingly valuable in the future job market. By developing this skill, you can enhance your productivity, wellbeing, and career prospects. The ability to stay focused on your goals and resist the constant barrage of distractions is a superpower in today's cluttered times. So, start your journey towards becoming indistractable today, and you'll be better prepared for the challenges and opportunities of the future workforce.

The stories of Sarah, Elon Musk, J.K. Rowling, and Tristan Harris demonstrate that indistractability is a skill that can significantly impact one's career and life. In today's cluttered times of social media and constant digital stimuli, the ability to stay focused and prioritise deep work is a valuable asset.

As we move forward into an uncertain future, where the job market continues to evolve, one thing remains constant: the need for individuals who can cut through the noise, stay indistractable, and make meaningful contributions to their fields. Whether you aspire to be a successful freelancer, a visionary CEO, a creative genius, or a tech advocate, mastering the art of indistractability will be your key to unlocking a future filled with opportunities and success.

Conversationality & Influenceability – Mastering the Global Language of Business

"Communicating is about connecting for lasting impact."

In a rapidly changing world where technology and automation continue to reshape the employment landscape, the ability to communicate effectively and influence others remains an invaluable skill. In this chapter, we will explore the essential skill of Conversationality & Influenceability – the art of conversing in the language of global business and capturing the attention of your audience. This skill is not just about speaking; it's about being understood, understanding others, and having the power to influence individuals and groups through your words, actions, and deeds.

The Power of Conversationality

In the digital age, the global language of business transcends borders and cultures. Whether you're an entrepreneur, a manager, or an employee, your ability to navigate the intricate web of business models, strategies, HR practices, finance principles, governance, and risk management is crucial. However, possessing knowledge alone is not enough. To truly thrive in the competitive world of business, you must also master the art of conversation.

Imagine a scenario in which two equally qualified candidates are competing for a high level executive position. Candidate A possesses exceptional technical skills and an in-depth understanding of business concepts. Candidate B, on the other hand, possesses these same skills but also excels in Conversationality. Candidate B can explain complex ideas with simplicity, engage in meaningful discussions, and create an atmosphere where others feel heard and valued.

In this situation, Candidate B is more likely to secure the position because they not only understand the language of business but also have the ability to converse fluently in it. This skill not only aids in daily interactions but also sets the stage for effective leadership and career advancement.

Real-Life Example: Elon Musk

One of the most prominent examples of someone who has mastered Conversationality and influenceability is Elon Musk, the CEO of Tesla and SpaceX. While Musk is known for his groundbreaking innovations and ambitious ventures, it's his ability to communicate his vision and ideas that has made him a global icon.

Musk's talent for public speaking allows him to articulate complex technological concepts to the public. He engages with his audience in a way that not only educates them but also sparks excitement and interest. His captivating presentations have helped attract investors, customers, and top talent to his companies.

Musk's influence goes beyond speeches; he leverages social media to communicate directly with the public and share updates on his projects. His tweets have the power to impact stock prices and influence public perception. It's not just what he says but how he says it that has made him a charismatic leader and influencer in the world of business and technology.

Developing Conversationality and Influenceability

To become an effective communicator and influencer, consider the following steps:

1. Study the Language of Business

   Begin by gaining a strong understanding of business models, strategies, HR practices, finance, governance, and risk management. Continuous learning in these areas will build your knowledge base and credibility.

2. Hone Your Public Speaking Skills

   Take courses in public speaking, attend workshops, and practice speaking in front of an audience. The ability to confidently present your ideas is a vital aspect of influenceability.

3. Listen Actively

   Effective communication is a two-way street. Practice active listening to understand the needs, concerns, and perspectives of others. This skill will enable you to tailor your message to your audience effectively.

4. Storytelling

   Learn the art of storytelling to make your messages relatable and memorable. People connect with narratives, so use stories to convey complex ideas in a compelling way.

5. Adapt to Your Audience

    Recognise that different situations and audiences require varying approaches. Adapt your communication style to suit the context and the individuals you are addressing.

6. Embrace Technology

    Leverage technology to enhance your reach and influence. Use social media, blogs, podcasts, and other digital platforms to connect with a wider audience and share your expertise.

Conversationality & Influenceability is a critical skill that can set you apart in the ever-evolving world of business. By mastering the global language of business, becoming an effective public speaker, and learning from influential figures like Elon Musk, you can harness the power of communication to advance your career and make a lasting impact on your professional journey.

Role Modelling & Self-Management: Building Trust for Future Success

*"Authenticity, consistency & self management
are the foundations for role modelling. "*

It is impossible to discern genuine from fake in social media today. Various influencers, mentors, and so-called role models parade their skill sets without adequate experience or knowledge. If you possess even an iota of authenticity and consistency, you will excel in the art of Role Modelling and Self-Management. This skill not only impacts your personal growth but also your ability to influence and lead others effectively in the ever-changing job market of the future.

The Essence of Role Modelling

Role Modelling isn't just about being a good example; it's about setting the highest standard for yourself and consistently living up to it. It involves demonstrating integrity, resilience, and a commitment to personal growth, which ultimately fosters trust in you among your peers and colleagues. Think of it as the beacon of hope and assurance that guides others through the uncertainties of the future.

One real-life example of Role Modelling comes from the world of business leadership: As the CEO of Apple, Tim Cook has demonstrated that leading one of the world's most valuable companies can be synonymous with ethical leadership and advocacy for privacy and environmental sustainability. Under his leadership, Apple has increased its commitment to renewable energy and has taken significant strides towards ensuring user privacy. Cook's approach to leadership, prioritising both profit and principle, serves as a model for future business leaders, emphasising that financial success can go hand-in-hand with ethical considerations.

The Importance of Self-Management

Self-Management goes hand-in-hand with Role Modelling. It is the practice of balance and restraint in all aspects of life, ensuring that you not only maintain your personal wellbeing but also inspire others to do the same. In an era marked by constant connectivity and the blurring of work and personal life, self-management becomes even more critical.

Consider the story of Angela, a young professional in the tech industry. Angela was known for her ability to manage her time effectively, maintain a healthy work-life balance, and exhibit calmness under pressure. Her colleagues admired her for her self-discipline and the sense of reassurance she provided during stressful times. Angela's consistent practice of self-management not only enhanced her own performance but also created a supportive work environment where her team felt empowered to do the same.

Building Trust and Followership

The skill of Role Modelling and Self-Management is a powerful tool for building trust and followership. When you demonstrate integrity, consistency, and resilience in your actions, people naturally gravitate towards you. They see you as a reliable source of guidance and inspiration in a world filled with uncertainty.

Take the example of Malala Yousafzai, the Pakistani activist who fought for girls' education. Her unwavering commitment to her cause, even in the face of adversity, made her a global symbol of resilience and hope. Malala's ability to manage herself emotionally and stay true to her mission earned her not only the Nobel Peace Prize but also millions of followers worldwide who continue to support her efforts.

The Future of Work and Role Modelling

As the job landscape continues to change, employers will seek individuals who not only possess technical skills but also excel in soft skills like Role Modelling and Self-Management. These skills will be the bedrock upon which successful careers are built, and they will be crucial for adapting to the ever-evolving demands of the workplace.

The skill of Role Modelling and Self-Management is an invaluable asset in the future job market. It not only benefits your personal growth and wellbeing but also allows you to inspire and lead others effectively. By embodying the principles of Role Modelling and Self-Management, you can build trust, followership, and a foundation for lasting success in a world of constant change.

The Power of Personal Credibility and Brand in Future Jobs

*"Credibility is about doing what you
say and only saying what you have done."*

We live in times characterised by rapidly evolving technology, shifting job landscapes, and constant information bombardment. One skill is set to become increasingly invaluable: building personal credibility and brand. As the world of work continues to transform, individuals who can establish themselves as trusted sources of information will not only secure their place in the job market but also become leaders in their respective fields. In this chapter, we will explore the significance of personal credibility and brand in future jobs and provide real-life examples of individuals who have mastered this skill to build remarkable careers.

The Currency of Trust

In the digital age, where information is abundant but trust is scarce, the ability to build personal credibility and brand has become a precious asset. Credibility is the foundation upon which trust is built, and trust is the currency of influence in today's interconnected world. Whether you are a leader within an organisation, an entrepreneur, or a freelancer, your credibility can open doors, drive opportunities, and shape your career trajectory.

Objective Curation of Information

One of the most potent ways to establish personal credibility and brand is through the objective curation of information. In a time when misinformation and fake news proliferate, individuals who can sift through the noise and present well-researched, balanced, and reliable information are highly valued.

Consider the example of Maria Rodriguez, a data scientist known for her meticulous curation of research reports related to artificial intelligence (AI) and machine learning. Maria recognised the growing demand for accurate AI insights and took it upon herself to curate the most relevant research papers, blogs, and articles in the field. She created a blog, "AI Insights by Maria," where she shared her curated findings, providing concise summaries and insightful commentary.

Maria's dedication to delivering objective and high-quality information made her a trusted resource in the AI community. Professionals, researchers, and even executives in AI-driven companies turned to her for guidance and updates. Over time, Maria's personal brand as a credible source of AI knowledge grew, leading to speaking invitations at conferences, consulting opportunities, and eventually, a book deal on the subject.

Building Credibility through Consistency

Another essential aspect of building personal credibility and brand is consistency. Whether you're curating news, writing blogs, or sharing insights, maintaining a regular presence is key to fostering trust and recognition. Consider the case of Mark Thompson, a cybersecurity expert. Mark started a weekly newsletter called "CyberWatch" that provided subscribers with the latest cybersecurity threats, best practices, and actionable advice. What set Mark apart was his unwavering commitment to delivering his newsletter every Friday without fail, rain or shine. As professionals and organisations across various industries subscribed to CyberWatch and shared its content within their networks, Mark's credibility as a cybersecurity expert soared. His consistency in providing valuable information built a loyal following and earned him a reputation as a go-to source for all things cybersecurity.

Leveraging Personal Credibility for Impact

Ultimately, personal credibility and brand are not just about personal recognition or career advancement; they are powerful tools for creating positive change and impact. Building credibility allows you to influence decisions, shape discussions, and drive meaningful conversations. Take the example of Sarah Chang, an environmental activist with a passion for sustainability. Sarah started by curating research reports, articles, and case studies related to climate change and sustainable practices. She shared her findings through her social media channels, gradually gaining followers who admired her dedication to environmental causes. As Sarah's credibility grew, she leveraged her influence to raise awareness about pressing environmental issues and advocate for policy changes. She collaborated with nonprofits, spoke at conferences, and even met with government officials to discuss sustainability initiatives. Through her tireless efforts, Sarah not only built a personal brand as a credible environmentalist but also contributed to meaningful change in her community and beyond.

In the world of future jobs, personal credibility and brand will be indispensable assets. The ability to curate objective information, maintain consistency, and leverage credibility for impact will distinguish individuals as respected sources of knowledge and leaders in their fields. As demonstrated by real-life examples like Maria Rodriguez, Mark Thompson, and Sarah Chang, building personal credibility and brand is not only a career-enhancing skill but also a pathway to making a positive difference in the world. In the chapters that follow, we will delve deeper into the practical strategies and techniques for cultivating these invaluable skills and achieving lasting success in the rapidly evolving job market of the future.

Eight Essential Skill Groups

"Common skills are the rarest to find."

There are several skills that are likely to be in high demand for future jobs. Here are eight key skill groups that are invaluable for a wide range of professions and have more or less been essential for success over the past few decades. They are described below with a deeper understanding of their importance in later chapters to provide context to today's times for each of these skill groups.

1. Technological literacy: As technology continues to advance, having a strong foundation in digital skills, including coding, data analysis, artificial intelligence, and cybersecurity, will be increasingly important.

2. Critical thinking and problem-solving: These skills involve the ability to analyse complex situations, think creatively, and find innovative solutions. Employers will seek individuals who can approach challenges with a logical and systematic mindset.

3. Adaptability and Flexibility: The future job market will require individuals who can quickly adapt to changing

circumstances and embrace new technologies and ways of working. Being open to learning and upskilling will be crucial.

4. Collaboration and teamwork: Effective collaboration across diverse teams and cultures is becoming more prevalent in the workplace. The ability to communicate, listen actively, and work well with others will be highly valued.

5. Emotional intelligence: With increased automation, roles that require human interaction, empathy, and emotional intelligence will be in-demand. Skills such as active listening, empathy, and understanding non-verbal cues will be valuable in professions like counselling, healthcare, and customer service.

6. Creativity and innovation: In an age of automation, creativity will remain a uniquely human skill. The ability to generate new ideas, think outside the box, and approach problems with a fresh perspective will be highly sought-after.

7. Cultural competence and diversity awareness: As the world becomes more interconnected, employers will seek individuals who can work effectively with diverse populations, understand cultural nuances, and navigate global markets.

8. Lifelong learning: With the rapid pace of technological advancements, the ability to learn new skills and adapt to new tools and techniques will be essential. Embracing a growth mindset and being committed to continuous learning will be crucial for future job success.

It's important to note that these skills are not limited to specific professions and can be valuable across various industries. The exact skills required may vary depending on the specific field or job role, but developing a strong foundation in these areas can position individuals well for the jobs of the future.

Cultivating Technological Literacy for the Future

"Technological literacy today is as vital as horse riding was in the 19th century, shaping the future as surely as mastering a saddle once conquered the past."

Automation, artificial intelligence, and digital technologies are becoming increasingly prevalent; technological literacy is no longer a mere advantage but a necessity. To stay competitive in the workforce of the future, individuals must not only embrace technology but also develop a deep understanding of it. In this chapter, we will explore what technological literacy entails, why it is vital, and how you can go about developing it.

Understanding Technological Literacy

Technological literacy is not limited to the ability to use everyday gadgets or software; it's about comprehending the fundamental principles and concepts behind technology and how they shape our world. It involves the capacity to think critically about technology, adapt to new digital tools, and leverage them effectively in various contexts. Here are some key components of technological literacy:

1. **Digital Literacy:** This encompasses basic computer skills, understanding operating systems, and proficiency with common software applications like word processors, spreadsheets, and presentation software.

2. **Coding and Programming:** Familiarity with coding languages such as Python, Java, or JavaScript can enable you to create, modify, and understand the inner workings of software and applications.

3. **Data Literacy:** As data becomes increasingly valuable, knowing how to gather, analyse, and interpret data is crucial. Tools like Microsoft Excel, data visualisation software, and statistical analysis techniques are essential.

4. **Cybersecurity Awareness:** Understanding the importance of online security and knowing how to protect your data and privacy is vital in today's digital landscape.

5. **AI and Machine Learning Awareness:** A grasp of the basics of artificial intelligence and machine learning will be invaluable, as these technologies become ubiquitous in various industries.

Why Technological Literacy Matters

Technological literacy is more than just a professional advantage; it's a life skill in the 21st century. Here are some reasons why it matters:

1. **Employability:** Many jobs now require at least a basic level of technological competence. As automation continues to rise, roles that involve human-technology interaction become increasingly critical.

2. **Problem-Solving:** A tech-savvy individual can approach problems with a broader toolkit, finding innovative solutions by leveraging digital tools and data analysis.

3. **Adaptability:** Technology evolves rapidly. Being technologically literate allows you to adapt to new tools and trends quickly, remaining relevant in the job market.

4. **Critical Thinking:** Understanding technology empowers you to question its ethical implications, make informed decisions about its use, and avoid falling victim to misinformation or scams.

Developing Technological Literacy

Now that we've established the importance of technological literacy, let's explore how you can develop and enhance this essential skill:

1. **Continuous Learning:** Embrace a growth mindset and be open to learning new technologies. Online courses, tutorials, and educational platforms like Coursera, edX, or Khan Academy can be invaluable resources.

2. **Practice:** Apply what you learn through hands-on experience. Experiment with coding, explore new software, or start a tech-related project.

3. **Stay Informed:** Follow tech news and trends through websites, podcasts, and social media. Engaging with the tech community can help you stay up-to-date.

4. **Join Tech Communities:** Attend meetups, join online forums, and participate in hackathons or coding challenges to connect with like-minded individuals and gain practical experience.

5. **Seek Mentors:**   Find mentors or advisers who are experts in technology-related fields. They can provide guidance and help you navigate the complex world of tech.

Examples of Technological Literacy in Action

Here are a few examples of individuals who have leveraged their technological literacy to succeed in the job market of the future:

1. **Jessica:**   A marketing manager who learned data analytics and used it to analyse customer behaviour, resulting in a 20% increase in conversion rates for her company's online campaigns.

2. **Carlos:**   A high school teacher who incorporated coding into his curriculum, enabling his students to develop problem-solving skills and prepare for future careers in technology.

3. **Maria:**   A cybersecurity enthusiast who identified and reported a security vulnerability in her company's software, earning recognition and a promotion.

4. **Ravi:**   A freelance writer who expanded his skill set to include content creation for virtual reality experiences, tapping into the growing demand for immersive storytelling.

Technological literacy is no longer optional—it's a core skill for thriving in the future job market. By understanding technology's fundamental principles, staying informed, and actively engaging with tech-related projects and communities, you can develop the proficiency needed to excel in the digital age. Embrace the opportunities technology offers and equip yourself for success in the evolving world of work.

Mastering Critical Thinking for Future-Proofing Your Career

"Critical thinking is the compass that guides us through complexity, the catalyst for innovation, and the foundation of informed decision-making."

In a rapidly changing world, where automation and artificial intelligence are reshaping the job landscape, one skill stands out as a beacon of adaptability and relevance: critical thinking. Critical thinking is the ability to analyse, evaluate, and synthesise information to make informed decisions and solve complex problems. In this chapter, we will explore the importance of critical thinking in future job markets, provide actionable strategies to develop this skill, and illustrate its application through real-world examples.

The Relevance of Critical Thinking in Future Jobs

As technology continues to advance, the demand for routine, manual tasks is decreasing, while the demand for cognitive skills, such as critical thinking, is on the rise. Critical thinking is essential for a wide range of professions, including data analysis, healthcare, law, finance, and more. Employers value employees who can think critically because they can:

1. Adapt to Change: Critical thinkers are flexible and open to new ideas, making them more resilient in the face of evolving job requirements and industry trends.

2. Solve Complex Problems: In an era of increasing complexity, those who can break down intricate problems into manageable components and devise creative solutions are highly sought-after.

3. Innovate and Drive Growth: Critical thinkers can identify opportunities for improvement and innovation, driving growth and competitiveness within organisations.

4. Make Informed Decisions: They are skilled at evaluating information, discerning credible sources, and making decisions based on evidence rather than emotion or bias.

Developing Critical Thinking Skills

Now, let's delve into practical strategies for developing and displaying critical thinking skills:

Cultivate Curiosity: Foster a mindset of curiosity by asking questions, seeking out new information, and exploring different perspectives on a topic.

1. Enhance Problem-Solving Abilities: Practice problem-solving by breaking issues into smaller parts, analysing causes and effects, and brainstorming solutions. Keep a journal to document your problem-solving process and its outcomes.

2. Develop Information Literacy: Learn to distinguish credible sources from unreliable ones. Evaluate information for bias, accuracy, and relevance to make informed decisions.

3. Engage in Socratic Questioning: Use Socratic questioning techniques to delve deeper into issues. Ask questions like "Why?" "What are the implications?" and "What evidence supports this?"

4. Embrace Critical Reading: When reading books, articles, or reports, actively engage with the material by highlighting key points, making annotations, and summarising the main ideas.

5. Seek Diverse Perspectives: Surround yourself with people who have different viewpoints and engage in constructive discussions and debates. Exposure to diverse perspectives enhances your critical thinking abilities.

Real-World Examples of Critical Thinking

Let's examine a few real-world examples of individuals who have effectively employed critical thinking in their careers:

1. **Elon Musk and SpaceX:** Elon Musk's vision to revolutionise space exploration through SpaceX required critical thinking at its core. His team had to evaluate existing space technologies, identify inefficiencies, and devise innovative solutions to reduce costs and make space more accessible.

2. **Dr. Anthony Fauci and Public Health:** During the COVID-19 pandemic, Dr. Fauci demonstrated exceptional critical thinking. He analysed evolving data, adapted

strategies based on emerging evidence, and communicated complex medical information to the public effectively.

3. **Warren Buffett and Investing:** Warren Buffett's success as an investor can be attributed to his rigorous analysis of companies and industries. His ability to critically evaluate financial statements and long-term prospects has made him one of the most successful investors in history.

Critical thinking is a skill that transcends industries and job roles. It is a key asset for future-proofing your career, enabling you to adapt, innovate, and excel in a changing world. By cultivating curiosity, honing problem-solving abilities, and embracing diverse perspectives, you can develop and display critical thinking skills that will set you apart in the job market of tomorrow. As demonstrated by the real-world examples, critical thinking is not just a theoretical concept; it is a tangible and valuable skill that can propel your career to new heights.

Cultivating Adaptability and Flexibility

*"Adaptability and flexibility are the keys
to humanity's survival and success."*

Rapid technological advancements, economic shifts, and unforeseen global events have made the ability to adapt and remain flexible more crucial than ever. Jobs and industries are evolving at an unprecedented pace, and those who can navigate these changes with agility are positioned for success. In this chapter, we will explore the importance of adaptability and flexibility and provide actionable strategies to develop these essential skills.

1. The Power of Adaptability and Flexibility

Adaptability and flexibility encompass the capacity to adjust, learn, and thrive in changing circumstances. These skills are not only desirable in the workplace but also fundamental for personal growth and resilience in an ever-shifting world. Let's dive into why they are so vital:

2. Future-Proofing Your Career:

The job landscape is constantly evolving, with emerging technologies and automation reshaping industries. Being adaptable and flexible ensures you can pivot and learn new skills, making yourself invaluable in any job market.

3. Handling Uncertainty:

Life is full of unpredictability. The COVID-19 pandemic is a prime example of how unforeseen events can disrupt our lives and careers. Developing adaptability equips you to face uncertainty with resilience.

4. Innovation and Problem-Solving:

Adaptability and flexibility are at the heart of innovation. Creative problem-solving often requires exploring new approaches and experimenting with unconventional ideas.

5. Effective Leadership:

Leaders who exhibit adaptability and flexibility inspire confidence in their teams. They can navigate change, guide their organisations through turbulent times, and foster a culture of growth.

6. Strategies to Develop Adaptability and Flexibility

Now that we understand the importance of these skills, let's explore practical ways to cultivate them:

7. Embrace a Growth Mindset:

Start by adopting a growth mindset, which involves believing in your ability to develop new skills and overcome challenges. Replace fixed beliefs with a mindset that welcomes change and sees setbacks as opportunities for growth.

Example: Microsoft's transformation from a software-focused company to a cloud computing leader under the leadership of CEO Satya Nadella is a testament to embracing change with a growth mindset.

8. Continual Learning:

Make lifelong learning a habit. Seek out courses, workshops, and online resources to acquire new skills. Stay curious and explore subjects outside your comfort zone.

Example: Consider the rise of Coursera and other online education platforms, enabling professionals to upskill and reskill in a wide range of fields.

9. Networking and Collaboration:

Build a diverse network of peers and mentors. Collaborating with individuals from various backgrounds can expose you to different perspectives and approaches, fostering adaptability.

Example: The open-source software community thrives on collaboration, with developers worldwide contributing to projects like Linux and TensorFlow.

10. Emulate Role Models:

Identify individuals who embody adaptability and flexibility in their careers. Study their journeys, learn from their experiences, and apply their principles to your own professional development.

Example: Elon Musk, with ventures spanning electric cars, space exploration, and neural technology, exemplifies adaptability in pursuing audacious goals.

11. Practice Resilience:

Develop resilience by facing adversity head-on. When setbacks occur, reflect on the experience, extract lessons, and use them to refine your approach in the future.

Example: The recovery and growth of New Orleans after Hurricane Katrina showcase the power of resilience and adaptability in rebuilding a city and its economy.

12. Adapt to Technological Changes:

Keep up with technological advancements relevant to your field. Embrace new tools and software to stay competitive and efficient.

Example: The integration of artificial intelligence and machine learning into healthcare is revolutionising patient care and medical research.

13. Seek Feedback and Self-Reflect:

Regularly solicit feedback from peers, supervisors, and self-assess your performance. Acknowledge areas for improvement and actively work on them.

Example: Agile software development methodologies promote continuous improvement through frequent feedback and adaptation.

In a world marked by constant change, the ability to adapt and remain flexible is your greatest asset. Whether you're preparing for the future job market, navigating personal challenges, or leading a team, the skills of adaptability and flexibility will guide you towards success. Embrace change as an opportunity for growth, and commit to a lifelong journey of learning and self-improvement. Remember, those who adapt thrive in the face of uncertainty, and they are the ones who shape the future.

Mastering Collaboration and Teamwork in the Era of Industry 4.0 and Remote Work

"Collaboration transcends borders and time zones, becoming the linchpin of innovation and success. By mastering communication, embracing diversity, and fostering trust, we unlock the true potential of teamwork in a digitally interconnected world."

In the fast-evolving world of Industry 4.0 and the rise of remote work, the ability to collaborate effectively and work as part of a team has become more critical than ever. The traditional boundaries of the workplace have dissolved, and now, professionals from across the globe can come together to achieve common goals. In this chapter, we will explore the skill of collaboration and teamwork in the context of the Fourth Industrial Revolution, offering insights, strategies, and examples to help you thrive in this new era.

The Changing Landscape

The Fourth Industrial Revolution, often referred to as Industry 4.0, is characterised by the integration of digital technologies, artificial intelligence, and automation into various aspects of work. As a result, jobs are becoming increasingly complex, requiring a diverse set of skills, including collaboration and teamwork. Furthermore, the rise of remote work has challenged traditional notions of teamwork, as teams are now often dispersed across different locations and time zones.

Developing Collaboration and Teamwork Skills

- Cultivate Effective Communication: Effective communication is the cornerstone of collaboration. In the digital age, mastering various communication tools is essential. Video conferencing, instant messaging, and project management software are just a few examples. It's crucial to know when to use each tool to facilitate clear and efficient communication.

  Example: The software development team at Company X utilises Slack for real-time messaging, Trello for project management, and holds weekly video meetings to discuss progress. This combination of tools helps them communicate effectively despite being spread across different countries.

- Embrace Diversity and Inclusion: Collaborative teams often consist of individuals from diverse backgrounds, cultures, and perspectives. Embracing this diversity can lead to more innovative solutions and better decision-making. Encourage open dialogue and actively seek input from all team members.

  Example: At Company Y, they intentionally form cross-functional teams consisting of members with different skill sets and backgrounds. This diversity has led to creative problem-solving and more inclusive decision-making processes.

- Set Clear Goals and Roles: In the era of remote work, team members must have a clear understanding of their roles and responsibilities. Setting specific goals and expectations helps prevent misunderstandings and promotes accountability.

  Example: Company Z uses project management software to define roles, set milestones, and track progress. This ensures that all team members understand their contributions and how they fit into the bigger picture.

- Foster Trust and Accountability: Trust is the foundation of effective teamwork. Team members must trust each other to deliver on commitments and be accountable for their actions. Building trust often takes time, but it's essential for long-term collaboration.

  Example: Team members at Company W regularly share their progress updates and openly discuss any challenges they face. This transparency helps build trust and allows for quick problem-solving.

- Adaptability and Flexibility: The ability to adapt to changing circumstances and work with agility is crucial in the digital age. Teams should be open to trying new approaches and continuously learning from their experiences.

  Example: Company A encourages its employees to attend regular workshops and training sessions to keep their skills up-to-date. This commitment to learning and adaptability has helped the team remain competitive in a rapidly changing industry.

Mastering collaboration and teamwork in the era of Industry 4.0 and remote work is essential for career success. By developing effective communication, embracing diversity, setting clear goals, fostering trust, and being adaptable, you can thrive in the ever-evolving landscape of work. The examples provided illustrate how organisations have successfully navigated these challenges and offer valuable insights for individuals looking to enhance their collaborative skills in this new era.

Imbibing Emotional Intelligence for Future-Proofing Your Career

"In a world where machines can replicate tasks, it is emotional intelligence that allows us to connect, empathize, and lead with humanity—qualities that no algorithm can imitate."

The importance of emotional intelligence cannot be overstated. As machines and algorithms continue to encroach on various industries, the skills that distinguish us as humans are becoming more vital than ever. Among these, emotional intelligence stands out as a quintessential ability for navigating the job landscape of the future.

Understanding Emotional Intelligence

Emotional intelligence, often abbreviated as EQ (Emotional Quotient), is the ability to recognise, understand, manage, and effectively use emotions, both our own and those of others. It encompasses a wide range of skills and traits, including self-awareness, self-regulation, empathy, social awareness, and relationship management. Developing these skills can help individuals excel in professions that require human interaction, empathy, and a deep understanding of emotional dynamics.

Why Emotional Intelligence Matters

As automation and artificial intelligence take over routine and repetitive tasks, jobs that necessitate human touch, empathy, and emotional intelligence are on the rise. Here's why EQ is indispensable in the workforce of the future:

- Enhanced Human Connection: In roles such as counselling, healthcare, and customer service, the ability to connect with people on an emotional level will be a differentiator. Clients, patients, or customers often seek emotional support and understanding, which only a human with developed emotional intelligence can provide.

- Conflict Resolution: Emotionally intelligent individuals are adept at resolving conflicts and managing disagreements effectively. In team settings, they can defuse tense situations, foster collaboration, and contribute to a more harmonious work environment.

- Adaptability: EQ allows individuals to adapt to rapidly changing situations and navigate ambiguity with ease. As industries evolve and new challenges emerge, emotionally intelligent professionals can thrive by quickly assessing and responding to shifting dynamics.

Developing Emotional Intelligence

Fortunately, emotional intelligence is a skill that can be nurtured and refined. Here are some strategies to help you develop your emotional intelligence:

- Self-Reflection: Start by increasing your self-awareness. Regularly reflect on your emotions, reactions, and triggers. Understand how your emotions affect your behaviour and decisions.

- Active Listening: Actively listen when others speak. Focus on their words, tone, and non-verbal cues. By doing so, you not only understand their perspectives better but also demonstrate empathy and respect.

- Empathy: Put yourself in others' shoes to understand their feelings and perspectives. Empathy allows you to connect on a deeper level and respond to their needs effectively.

- Non-Verbal Communication: Pay attention to non-verbal cues such as facial expressions, body language, and gestures. These can convey emotions and thoughts that words alone might not express.

- Practice Self-Regulation: Learn to manage your emotions, especially in high-stress situations. Techniques like mindfulness, deep breathing, and meditation can help you stay calm and composed.

- Seek Feedback: Solicit feedback from colleagues, friends, or mentors about your emotional intelligence. They can provide valuable insights into areas where you can improve.

Real-World Examples

Let's explore some real-world examples of how emotional intelligence is vital in various professions:

- Healthcare: Doctors with high EQ can better empathise with patients, comfort them during difficult diagnoses, and improve patient compliance with treatment plans.

- Counselling: Therapists with strong emotional intelligence can establish trust and rapport with clients, facilitating more productive therapy sessions.

- Customer Service: Customer service representatives who listen attentively, show empathy, and handle irate customers with patience can turn negative experiences into positive ones.

Emotional intelligence is a skill that will become increasingly valuable in future job markets. By honing your emotional intelligence, you can stand out in your profession, build meaningful connections, and contribute to a more compassionate and empathetic workplace. As the world becomes more automated, it is our ability to understand and connect with others on an emotional level that will truly set us apart.

Unleashing Creativity and Innovation in an Age of Automation

"Creativity is the compass that guides us through the dynamic landscape of the modern workforce, illuminating paths that machines cannot tread and opening doors to infinite possibilities."

The skill of creativity and innovation has emerged as a beacon of hope for individuals seeking not just job security, but also professional fulfilment. While robots and algorithms excel at repetitive tasks and data analysis, they still struggle to replicate the boundless imagination, intuitive leaps, and fresh insights that humans can generate. In this chapter, we will explore the importance of creativity in the modern workforce, delve into strategies for nurturing your creative abilities, and present real-world examples of individuals who have harnessed their creativity to carve out successful careers in various fields.

Why Creativity Matters

Imagine a future where machines can efficiently handle routine tasks, analyse data, and perform repetitive jobs with unmatched precision. While this may sound like a utopian vision, it also raises a pressing question: What role will humans play in such a world?

The answer lies in our ability to be creative and innovative. Creativity is not limited to artistic pursuits; it encompasses the capacity to generate fresh ideas, solve complex problems, and envision novel solutions across all domains. Here's why it matters:

- Problem-Solving: Creative thinkers approach problems differently, often discovering unconventional solutions that machines might overlook. When faced with unexpected challenges, individuals who can think outside the box are invaluable assets to any organisation.

- Adaptability: The pace of technological change means that the skills required for a job today may become obsolete tomorrow. Creativity allows individuals to adapt to new situations, acquire new skills, and pivot in their careers.

- Entrepreneurship: Creative thinkers are more likely to identify market gaps and create innovative products or services. Entrepreneurs who harness their creativity can build thriving businesses that disrupt entire industries.

Developing Creativity and Innovation

Creativity is not a fixed trait; it's a skill that can be nurtured and cultivated. Here are some strategies to develop your creative abilities:

- Embrace Curiosity: Cultivate a curious mindset. Ask questions, explore diverse subjects, and seek out new experiences. Curiosity is the foundation of creativity.

- Break Routines: Challenge your daily routines and comfort zones. Novel experiences and environments can stimulate your brain and inspire fresh ideas.

- Collaborate and Diversify: Interact with people from different backgrounds and disciplines. Collaboration with diverse teams often leads to more innovative solutions as it combines varied perspectives and expertise.

- Practice Mindfulness: Mindfulness techniques can help quiet your mind, reduce stress, and promote creative thinking. Meditation, for example, can enhance your ability to focus and generate ideas.

- Exercise Creativity: Engage in creative hobbies, whether it's painting, writing, or cooking. These activities not only provide an outlet for creativity but also enhance your overall imaginative abilities.

Real-World Examples

- Steve Jobs, co-founder of Apple Inc. Jobs was known for his remarkable ability to foresee future trends in technology and his relentless pursuit of innovation and excellence. His creative thinking was not just limited to technological innovation but also extended to product design, marketing, and branding. Steve Jobs introduced the concept of integrating aesthetics and functionality in electronic products, which was revolutionary at the time. Under his leadership, Apple launched groundbreaking products like the iPod, iPhone, and iPad, which not only transformed the technology industry but also how people interact with technology in their daily lives. His approach to creating user-friendly products with sleek, minimalist design has set new standards in product design across industries. Furthermore, Jobs was a master storyteller and marketer. He knew how to present Apple products in a way that captivated audiences and created unparalleled brand loyalty. His keynote speeches, where he introduced new products, became iconic for their presentation style and the excitement they generated. Steve Jobs' creative vision and ability to innovate across multiple facets of business operations have left a lasting legacy in the tech industry and beyond, making him a quintessential example of applying creative thinking in business.

- Gitanjali Rao: This young innovator was named *Time* magazine's Kid of the Year in 2020 for her remarkable inventions. At just 15, she developed a device to detect lead in water, showcasing how a creative approach to problem-solving can have a real impact on society.

- IDEO: This renowned design and innovation consultancy firm employs a diverse team of creative thinkers from various fields. Their collaborative and user-centred approach to problem-solving has led to the creation of innovative products and services for clients around the world.

As automation continues to reshape the job market, creativity and innovation are becoming more critical than ever. Embracing creativity as a skill and adopting strategies to nurture it can not only secure your place in the workforce but also lead to a more fulfilling and impactful career. The future belongs to those who can think beyond the confines of algorithms and embrace the limitless possibilities of the human imagination.

Developing Cultural Competence and Diversity Awareness

"In today's interconnected world, embracing cultural competence and diversity awareness is not just a professional necessity—it's a catalyst for innovation, empathy, and global success."

In a rapidly globalising world, the ability to work effectively with people from diverse backgrounds and cultures has become an essential skill for future jobs. Employers are increasingly seeking individuals who can not only tolerate differences but also leverage them to drive innovation, creativity, and productivity. In this chapter, we will explore the importance of cultural competence and diversity awareness and provide practical strategies and examples to develop and enhance these crucial skills.

Understanding Cultural Competence and Diversity Awareness

Cultural competence refers to the ability to interact and communicate effectively with people from different cultural backgrounds. It involves recognising, respecting, and valuing the unique characteristics and perspectives of individuals from diverse cultures. Diversity awareness, on the other hand, encompasses being aware of, acknowledging, and appreciating the differences in race, ethnicity, gender, age, religion, sexual orientation, and more.

Why Cultural Competence and Diversity Awareness Matter

1. Globalisation and Interconnectedness: As businesses expand globally, employees often work with colleagues, clients, and partners from different cultural backgrounds. Understanding cultural nuances can help avoid misunderstandings, miscommunications, and conflicts.

2. Innovation and Creativity: Diverse teams bring together a variety of perspectives, which can lead to more innovative solutions and creative ideas. Cultural competence enables individuals to collaborate effectively in diverse teams, driving organisational success.

3. Market Expansion: Companies operating in global markets need employees who can relate to and understand the needs and preferences of customers from different cultures. This can lead to more effective marketing and product development.

4. Legal and Ethical Considerations: Many countries have laws and regulations related to diversity and inclusion. Organisations must ensure they comply with these laws and promote diversity in the workplace to avoid legal issues and reputation damage.

Developing Cultural Competence and Diversity Awareness

1. Cultural Education and Training: Invest in cultural competency training programmes and workshops. These can provide insights into different cultures, help develop empathy, and foster understanding.

Example: A multinational corporation offers employees online courses on cultural competency, encouraging them to gain a deeper understanding of various cultures. These courses include real-life case studies and scenarios to apply what they've learned.

2. Travel and Exposure: Travelling to different countries and immersing oneself in different cultures is a powerful way to develop cultural competence. However, if international travel is not possible, try attending cultural events, festivals, or local community gatherings.

   Example: A software developer with an interest in Japanese culture takes a vacation to Japan, learns the language, and participates in local traditions. This experience broadens their cultural understanding and helps them relate better to Japanese colleagues.

3. Active Listening and Empathy: Practice active listening to understand others' perspectives. Empathy, the ability to feel and understand another person's experiences, is key to diversity awareness.

   Example: A manager listens attentively to an employee's concerns about workplace inclusivity. The manager acknowledges the employee's feelings and commits to addressing the issues raised.

4. Diverse Networking: Build a network of colleagues, mentors, and friends from diverse backgrounds. Engaging in conversations and seeking advice from people with different experiences can expand your cultural awareness.

   Example: A college student joins a multicultural student association and makes friends with peers from various countries. Through these friendships, they learn about different cultures and perspectives.

5. Continuous Learning: Keep up with global events, trends, and developments related to diversity and inclusion. Books, podcasts, and online resources can provide valuable insights.

    Example: A marketing professional regularly reads books on global marketing and diversity trends to stay informed and apply this knowledge to their work.

Cultural competence and diversity awareness are essential skills for thriving in the interconnected world of future jobs. By embracing these skills, you not only become a more valuable asset to employers but also contribute to a more inclusive and innovative society. Remember that developing these skills is an ongoing process, and the more you practice and learn, the better equipped you will be to navigate diverse and dynamic global markets.

Lifelong Learning: Navigating the Ever-Changing Landscape

"Unlearning disrupts the status quo and pushes us out of our comfort zones—yet it is the crucial lifeline to achieving future success."

In a world where the only constant is change, the ability to learn, unlearn, and relearn has never been more critical. The rapid pace of technological advancements, coupled with evolving market dynamics, is reshaping the employment landscape at an unprecedented rate. To stay relevant and succeed in future jobs, individuals must develop the skill of lifelong learning.

The Necessity of Lifelong Learning

The concept of lifelong learning has moved from a nice-to-have trait to an absolute necessity in the contemporary job market. Gone are the days when you could acquire a set of skills and rely on them throughout your entire career. Today, the skills that are in-demand can change in a matter of months, making adaptability and continuous learning indispensable.

Consider the case of the software developer who mastered a programming language in their early career. In the past, they might have expected to apply that skill for decades. However, with the relentless evolution of technology, that language might become obsolete within a few years. To stay competitive, this developer must be prepared to embrace new languages, frameworks, and methodologies.

The Growth Mindset

Developing the skill of lifelong learning begins with cultivating a growth mindset. Psychologist Carol Dweck introduced the idea of fixed and growth mindsets. A fixed mindset believes that abilities and intelligence are static, while a growth mindset thrives on challenges and sees failures as opportunities for growth.

Embracing a growth mindset means acknowledging that you can always improve and adapt. It involves being open to new ideas, seeking out challenges, and persisting in the face of setbacks. This mindset forms the foundation for successful lifelong learning.

Strategies for Lifelong Learning

- Set Clear Goals: Define your learning objectives and identify the skills you want to acquire or improve. Having clear goals will help you stay focused and motivated.

- Stay Curious: Cultivate a natural curiosity about the world around you. Ask questions, seek out information, and explore topics that pique your interest.

- Diversify Your Sources: Don't limit yourself to a single source of knowledge. Utilise a variety of resources such as books, online courses, podcasts, mentors, and industry conferences to gather information and perspectives.

- Structured Learning: Consider enrolling in formal courses or programmes that align with your career goals. Online platforms like Coursera, edX, and LinkedIn Learning offer a plethora of options for skill development.

- Practice Regularly: Apply what you've learned through practical projects and exercises. Active learning helps solidify new skills and knowledge.

- Feedback and Reflection: Seek feedback from peers or mentors to identify areas for improvement. Reflect on your experiences and learn from both successes and failures.

Real-World Examples

1. Ray Dalio

Ray Dalio stands out as a prime example of someone who has applied lifelong learning in business outside of the often-mentioned figures like Elon Musk, Jeff Bezos, and Warren Buffett. Dalio is the founder of Bridgewater Associates, the world's largest hedge fund. His commitment to principles and radical transparency within his company showcases his dedication to continuous learning and improvement.

Dalio has openly shared his journey of learning and personal development through his writings and public speaking. In his book, "Principles: Life and Work," he details the foundational beliefs that guided him in both life and business, emphasising the importance of understanding the natural order of things and learning from one's mistakes. He advocates for a culture of open-mindedness and asserts that the key to success is not only in having the right answers but in asking the right questions.

Dalio's approach to business is deeply rooted in his belief in radical truth and radical transparency, encouraging thoughtful disagreements and making it safe to express unconventional ideas. This culture of openness and rigorous testing of ideas is indicative of Dalio's lifelong learning philosophy, where feedback is seen as a valuable opportunity for growth and improvement.

Dalio has invested in creating tools and processes that facilitate personal development and learning within Bridgewater, such as the "Dot Collector" system, which collects real-time feedback during meetings to help improve decision-making and personal growth. This system reflects Dalio's belief in the power of data and feedback in fostering learning and development.

Dalio's journey is a testament to how lifelong learning can be effectively applied in business to create a culture of continuous improvement and innovation. His principles and practices demonstrate the impact of embracing learning as an ongoing process, not just for personal growth but as a cornerstone of organisational success.

2. *Angela Merkel*

Angela Merkel, the former Chancellor of Germany, holds a Ph.D. in quantum chemistry. Despite her extensive academic background, she demonstrated a commitment to lifelong learning by adapting to the ever-evolving political landscape. Her ability to navigate complex international issues and lead effectively for 16 years is a testament to her adaptability and open-mindedness.

In a world where the jobs of tomorrow are unknown, the skill of lifelong learning is your compass and anchor. It's not just about acquiring new skills; it's about embracing change, staying curious, and cultivating a mindset that thrives on growth and adaptation. By following the strategies outlined in this chapter and drawing inspiration from real-world examples, you'll be better equipped to navigate the ever-changing landscape of future jobs and thrive in an age of rapid technological advancement. Remember, it's not about what you know today; it's about your willingness to learn what you don't know tomorrow.

Part 3

FUTURE JOBS & CAREERS

"The precise jobs and careers of the future may be uncertain, but by connecting the dots the wise can deduce the direction they are headed in."

Future Jobs

"The future of jobs has already arrived;
we just need to shift our focus to the right sectors."

Predicting the specific nature of future jobs with precision is a challenging task, limited to broad categories such as artificial intelligence, healthcare, and personalised services. However, by analysing current trends and indicators, we can make educated guesses about the types of jobs that will emerge in the next ten to twenty years. The actual rate and volume of job creation will depend on a myriad of factors, including market demand, the speed of societal transformation, technological innovation rates, and an array of other social, economic, and technological elements.

There are hardly any degree-based courses for these jobs, and they mostly fall in the cusp of diverse skills and intersection of diverse experiences. It is precisely this that will create a demand-supply gap leading to disproportionate compensation for these jobs. Early adopters and risk-takers will be rewarded with fast-tracked careers and future roles as mentors in these careers much before they could dream of such status and compensation in traditional career paths.

Some of the jobs that are visible in the foreseeable future make for fascinating reading and seem whacky at first glance, but think deeper, and you will make sense in relation to what is happening around you socially, economically, and technologically.

In the relentless pursuit of academic excellence, universities find themselves at a crossroads, stuck in the comfortable cocoon of disseminating knowledge while the world hurtles towards the Industry 4.0 revolution. The traditional model of education, centred around curriculum-driven teaching, is increasingly at odds with the dynamic demands of the modern workforce.

As the Fourth Industrial Revolution reshapes industries, universities remain anchored in an era where knowledge was power. While they continue to produce graduates armed with theoretical prowess, the chasm between academia and industry widens. The industry now hungers not for mere information regurgitators but for skilled professionals equipped with competencies tailored for the digital age.

In the epoch of Industry 4.0, where artificial intelligence, robotics, and data analytics reign supreme, universities must evolve from being knowledge dispensers to skill cultivators. The incessant drumbeat of change demands a departure from the rigid confines of traditional curricula. Instead, universities must embrace agility, fostering an environment that nurtures innovation, critical thinking, and adaptability.

The call is not to abandon the foundation of knowledge but to transcend it. Industry 4.0 requires a symbiosis between academia and the corporate realm, where universities become dynamic hubs incubating the skills essential for the future. It's time for an education revolution, breaking free from the antiquated chains of rote learning and embarking on a journey that aligns education with the needs of Industry 4.0. Until then, universities risk becoming relics in the rearview mirror of progress, disconnected from the very revolution they should be spearheading.

As we navigate the ever-evolving landscape of technology, artificial intelligence, and a rapidly changing global economy, the job market is also undergoing a transformation. Traditional career paths are giving way to a host of unconventional jobs that were once considered futuristic fantasies. These are just some of the unconventional jobs of the future, driven by technological advancements and societal shifts. Are the universities equipping the future workforce to deliver these roles?

Future Jobs till 2030

There's no question that technology has evolved exponentially in the past few years than at any other time in history. At this rate, it wouldn't be far-fetched to expect it to progress by bigger leaps and bounds in the years to come. Futurists and job trend experts have mulled over what the future jobs market will look like, and here's their consensus about what the top jobs of the future 2025-2030 will be.

- *Work-from-Home Coordinator*

  Among the jobs of the future on this list, this is one that is probably seeing the biggest demand today. The COVID-19 pandemic compelled many companies and businesses to allow their employees to work-from-home, and now that restrictions have been lifted in many areas, more than half of those who have been working remotely say that they want to continue with the setup.

To optimise the work-from-home experience, companies have begun to hire people who can become the point of contact for their remote employees. As more and more organisations see the benefit of remote work, expect the demand for this relatively new job designation to grow further in the immediate future.

- *Smart Home Designer*

Households are increasingly harnessing the power of connectivity and smart applications in their devices and appliances. But maximising the benefits of smart home appliances requires time, patience, and a learning curve—which means some people can do with an expert to help them set up their smart systems accordingly. Enter the smart home designer, who helps homeowners manage their entire home with modern and connected home solutions.

Much like an interior designer, smart home designers create drawing blueprints, except theirs include structured wiring networks and a detailed description of how devices interact with each other. They handle systems such as home theatres, landscape lighting, outdoor lighting and audio, climate control, and security systems, among many others. Requirements for these jobs of the future include a background in interior design, along with sufficient and regularly updated training in modern home appliances and systems.

- *Digital Currency Adviser*

As the financial world shifts its interest towards cryptocurrency, those investing in the likes of Bitcoin, Litecoin, and ether will need the expertise of a digital currency adviser who can best steer their investments to success. Digital currency advisers are masters of cryptocurrencies and can teach investors how to manage their digital wealth. Aside from an essential background in accounting and financial management, applicants for these future jobs should also have a firm grasp of data security and encryption.

- *Spacecraft Pilot*

The modern space race is on. Following the launch of the so-called Space Force, Elon Musk and Jeff Bezos, the two richest men in the world, are trying to one-up each other to become the world's first commercial space transportation provider. Ultimately, this means that demand for spacecraft pilots will soar, no pun intended. As with any pilot job, the most important qualification for applying for spacecraft pilot jobs of the future (2025) is logging a good number of flight hours. This must then be coupled with a solid background in outer space-related majors such as astronomy, astrophysics, and astronautics.

- *Rewilder*

As the name suggests, rewilders are in charge of combining the urban jungle with elements of the real one. There's no question that the industrial revolution has largely been harmful to nature, and rewilders are tasked with reversing the trend by introducing forests and native species to abandoned factories, decrepit buildings, and other unused infrastructure. Aside from a background in urban planning, rewilder jobs of the future (2025) must entail advanced degrees in agriculture, environmental science, wildlife management, and the like.

- *Extinct Species Revivalist*

The science fiction movie Jurassic Park may soon be science fiction no more. With an estimated 200 to 2,000 species dying off each year, things are only about to get worse, as climate change is expected to double these death rate numbers by 2040. The good news is that, much like in the Steven Spielberg-helmed flick, the technology now exists to revive extinct species. Suffice to say, in the very near future, extinct species revivalists will not only be able to bring dead species back to life, but also reintroduce them to their natural habitats.

Those who want to apply for extinct species revivalist jobs in 2025 will need a strong background in the natural sciences such as biology, chemistry, and medicine, much like rewilder jobs in 2025. This must then be combined with additional studies on the geographical, ethical, and legal concerns that govern each revived species in order to be successful at these jobs that will be in-demand in 2025.

- *Care Provider for the Elderly*

By 2030, all members of the baby boomer generation will be over 65, the age that most industrialised Western nations consider as a senior. Technological advances in health and medicine are helping people live longer, making senior care the biggest social concern of the future.

With this in mind, care providers for the elderly jobs in 2030 will be asked to do more than just take care of the daily chores for their respective senior patients. The scope of responsibilities will likely extend to listening to them, cheering them up, providing advice, and other forms of care expected of a life companion. That's why the term "care provider for the elderly" is increasingly being replaced with the more appropriate "companion for the aged" for these jobs in 2030.

If you think that this is a career path you might want to take, some of the key competencies necessary for these jobs that will be in-demand in 2030 include empathy, patience, and being observant to see if the elderly person in your care is experiencing any emotional distress, anxiety, or depression.

- *AI Specialist*

Thanks to the many applications of artificial intelligence (AI) in practically all industries, AI Specialists are blessed with many routes to choose from—from automation to robotics to computer programming and app development, and other fields relating to math, engineering, technology, and so on. As for the jobs themselves, AI specialists have a number of roles to fill, including software development, research science, algorithm programming, data engineering, and even AI consultancy. To be considered qualified for these future jobs in 2025, one must enter into degree programmes that offer specific majors in AI. Another avenue is to pursue an AI specialisation from within majors such as engineering, computer science, information technology, and the like.

- *Data Detective*

As data usage and storage continue to evolve in today's digital age, data analysis as a career can only grow in importance. By 2025, experts are forecasting that nearly 30 percent of data generated will be real-time, thereby requiring faster and more efficient computing from both the men and machines that use them. Data detectives serve as experts who follow the trail of data and can serve in different areas of information technology such as data recovery and data forensics.

More than simple data processing and analysis, studied data will also need to be translated into terms that will be easy for the layman to understand, and data detectives can also serve this function. Aside from typical data analysing, data detective future jobs in 2030 also need to develop an investigative problem-solving mentality and demonstrate a keen understanding of a wide array of data-related issues plaguing today's data systems and networks.

Future Job Sectors

"The curious will rule the world."

The future job market is constantly evolving due to advances in technology, changes in societal needs, and emerging industries. While it's difficult to predict the exact jobs that will dominate in the future, there are several fields that are expected to see significant growth and demand. Here are some potential jobs of the future:

- Artificial Intelligence (AI) Specialist: As AI continues to advance, there will be a growing need for professionals who can develop, implement, and maintain AI systems and algorithms.

- Data Scientist: With the increasing reliance on data-driven decision-making, data scientists will play a crucial role in analysing and interpreting complex data to extract valuable insights and drive business strategies.

- Virtual Reality (VR)/Augmented Reality (AR) Developer: VR and AR technologies are expected to become more prevalent across various industries, creating a demand for developers skilled in creating immersive experiences and applications.

- Sustainability Manager: As environmental concerns become more pressing, sustainability managers will be responsible for implementing eco-friendly practices and ensuring organisations comply with environmental regulations.

- Genetic Counsellor: The field of genetics and personalised medicine is rapidly advancing. Genetic counsellors will guide individuals and families in understanding their genetic information and making informed decisions about their health.

- Cybersecurity Specialist: With the increasing frequency of cyber threats and data breaches, cybersecurity professionals will be crucial in safeguarding sensitive information and developing robust security measures.

- Drone Operator/Manager: Drones are being used in various industries, including delivery services, agriculture, and infrastructure inspection. Drone operators and managers will be needed to oversee their operations.

- Blockchain Developer: Blockchain technology is gaining traction, particularly in finance and supply chain industries. Blockchain developers will be responsible for creating and implementing secure decentralised systems.

- Digital Marketing Specialist: With the rise of online platforms, businesses will require experts who can navigate the digital landscape, develop effective marketing strategies, and utilise data analytics for targeted advertising.

- Healthcare Technologist: The healthcare industry will continue to incorporate technology for improved patient care and diagnostics. Healthcare technologists will be skilled in managing and maintaining medical devices and systems.

It's important to note that the jobs of the future will likely require a combination of technical skills, adaptability, and a willingness to continuously learn and update one's knowledge to keep pace with the changing job market.

Some Unconventional Jobs of the Future

"Unconventional future jobs will be at the intersection of technology and where imagination meets necessity."

Unconventional jobs of the future will likely emerge from technological advancements, environmental challenges, and evolving societal needs. Some of these jobs might include virtual reality (VR) experience designers, who craft immersive digital environments for education, training, and entertainment. With the growth of the metaverse, demand for professionals adept at creating and managing these virtual spaces will rise. Additionally, climate change will spur the need for roles like climate adaptation specialists, who develop strategies to help communities and businesses mitigate and adapt to environmental impacts.

Another unconventional job might be a digital currency advisor. As cryptocurrencies and blockchain technologies become more mainstream, individuals and businesses will require expert guidance on investments, transactions, and regulatory compliance. Similarly, biohacker consultants could emerge, helping people optimize their health and performance using cutting-edge biotech solutions.

To spot trends towards these jobs, it's crucial to monitor advancements in technology, environmental policies, and social behaviours. Keeping an eye on research publications, attending industry conferences, and engaging with thought leaders on platforms like LinkedIn can provide insights into emerging fields. Additionally, tracking venture capital investments and startup activities can highlight which industries are poised for growth, signalling the potential for new, unconventional job opportunities.

- *Smart Home Designer*

  With homes increasingly becoming connected, the demand for smart home designers can only grow. Even today, smart home companies are hiring Smart Home System Designers who have the right combination of deep technical knowledge, creativity, and practicality to help homeowners maximise the benefits they get from their smart home systems.

- *Work-from-Home Facilitator*

  Although many employees were forced to work-from-home during the height of the pandemic, a stunning 82 percent actually prefer to stay in the setup than to go back to an office. That's why companies are scrambling to hire Work-From-Home Facilitators to supply remote workers with the support they need—whether it involves communication, tools for work, or even following up on their wellbeing—to help them do their best work.

- *Workplace Environment Designer*

  Of course, organisations also need to give office workers attention as much as they do their work-from-home counterparts. With the pandemic causing many companies to rethink their office architecture, Workplace Environment Designers will play a major role in ensuring employee wellbeing and enjoyment in the years ahead.

- *Distraction Prevention Coach*

  This professional will serve as psychological help for people who can't seem to separate themselves from their smartphones, especially at work. By having a Distraction Prevention Coach, companies can steer their employees' attention back to their work instead of losing themselves in their smartphone obsession. Some of the requirements for this job will be a degree in human resources and/or psychology, as well as any relevant accreditation.

- *Wellbeing Director*

  The modern workplace brings with it all new kinds of stressors for the workers of the future, and the Wellbeing Director is tasked with addressing employees' mental, physical, emotional, and spiritual health to ensure productivity is maintained and burnout is prevented. Acting like a psychologist, yoga instructor, and spiritual adviser rolled into one, the people in these future jobs must create solutions that address employee stress, isolation, and conflict, among many other workplace-related issues.

- *Algorithm Bias Auditor*

  Companies today are placing higher importance on equality and inclusivity, and as the job title suggests, Algorithm Bias Auditors are there to ensure cognitive technologies are free from bias and discrimination. They help tweak algorithms to achieve equal opportunity for data users and work to ensure the fairness of the workforce. Requirements of these jobs of the future (2050 and beyond) include an advanced degree in ethics and bias management, and keen IT knowledge.

- *Human Bias Auditor*

Human Bias Auditors work closely with Algorithm Bias Auditors and other decision-makers to remove bias in all business functions overseen by HR. The focus of these future jobs is to achieve fair treatment of employees irrespective of gender, race, culture, civil status, age, etc. Similar to Algorithm Bias Auditors, Human Bias Auditors are also required to have a substantial background in ethics and bias management, as well as an advanced degree in fields related to HR.

- *Man-Machine Teaming Manager*

Pretty soon, man and machine will be working together, and there lies the need for a system of communication and collaboration between the two. This is the responsibility that these future jobs must fulfill.

- *Tidewater Architect*

With the sea level expected to rise 10 to 12 inches in the next 30 years, Tidewater Architects could soon be the biggest heroes of the jobs of the future 2050 and beyond. These professionals are projected to take on massive civil projects to address the many challenges of global warming and climate change.

- *Chief Purpose Planner*

Organisations need vision to thrive, and a Chief Purpose Planner will help companies develop a corporate purpose, along with strategies and narratives that serve that purpose. A solid HR background, along with in-depth knowledge of corporate ethics, social media behaviour, and employee/client engagement, are prerequisites of these future jobs.

- *Virtual Reality Architect*

  With the continued development of virtual reality (VR) and augmented reality (AR) technologies, a new breed of professionals is emerging – virtual reality architects. These individuals design immersive virtual spaces for various purposes, such as virtual meetings, educational experiences, and entertainment. Virtual reality architects combine skills in architecture, design, and programming to create interactive and realistic virtual environments.

- *Drone Traffic Controller*

  As drone technology becomes more integrated into various industries, the need for drone traffic controllers is likely to rise. These professionals would manage the flow of drone traffic in urban and rural areas, ensuring safe and efficient operation. Similar to air traffic controllers, drone traffic controllers would use advanced systems to monitor and coordinate drone movements, preventing collisions and optimising routes.

- *AI Ethics Consultant*

  As artificial intelligence plays an increasingly prominent role in decision-making processes, the demand for AI ethics consultants is likely to grow. These professionals would be responsible for ensuring that AI systems operate ethically and without bias. They would assess and address the ethical implications of AI algorithms, making recommendations to developers and organisations to promote responsible AI use.

- *Quantum Computing Engineer*

  Quantum computing is on the horizon, promising unprecedented computational power. Quantum computing engineers will be at the forefront of this technological revolution, designing, building, and maintaining quantum computers. These professionals will need a deep understanding of quantum mechanics and information theory, ushering in a new era of computing capabilities.

- *Space Tourism Guide*

  As space tourism becomes a reality, a new industry of space tourism guides may emerge. These guides would accompany civilians on space journeys, providing information about the spacecraft, ensuring passenger safety, and offering insights into the wonders of space. Space tourism guides would need a combination of space science knowledge, customer service skills, and training for handling space travel-related challenges.

- *Urban Agriculturist*

  With increasing urbanisation and a growing emphasis on sustainable living, urban agriculturists may become vital members of future communities. These individuals would design and manage urban farming systems, integrating agriculture into city landscapes. Urban agriculturists would contribute to local food production, promote environmental sustainability, and enhance the overall quality of urban life.

- *Personal Branding Consultant for AI Influencers*

  As AI-driven influencers become more prevalent on social media, a new profession may emerge: personal branding consultants for AI influencers. These consultants would help individuals and businesses develop and manage the online personas of their AI-generated influencers, ensuring they connect with their target audience and align with the desired brand image.

The job market of the future is set to be filled with unconventional opportunities that align with technological advancements and societal changes. Embracing these emerging roles will require a dynamic approach to education and skill development, as well as a willingness to adapt to the ever-shifting landscape of the modern workforce. As we look ahead, it's clear that the jobs of the future will be as diverse and innovative as the technologies that drive them.

Likely Highest Paying Jobs of the Future

"The highest-paying jobs of the future will blend technological proficiency with human judgment, leveraging our unique ability to think creatively, ethically, and strategically."

The highest-paying jobs of the future are expected to be those that require advanced expertise and human judgement. As technology continues to evolve, areas where human intuition, creativity, and decision-making are critical will become increasingly valuable. Key sectors likely to see high-paying roles include technology, healthcare, and finance.

In technology, roles such as artificial intelligence (AI) specialists, data scientists, and cybersecurity experts will be in high demand. AI specialists will be crucial for developing and managing intelligent systems that can learn and adapt. Despite the rise of AI, human judgement will be essential to address ethical concerns, make strategic decisions, and ensure these systems align with societal values.

Healthcare will also see significant growth in high-paying jobs, especially in roles like medical researchers, biotech engineers, and personalised medicine specialists. These positions require deep scientific knowledge and the ability to make complex decisions about patient care and treatment innovations. Human judgement is vital in interpreting medical data, understanding patient needs, and making life-saving decisions.

In finance, the future will demand more quantitative analysts, investment managers, and financial advisors. While algorithms can process vast amounts of data, human judgement is indispensable for understanding market trends, assessing risks, and making investment decisions that consider both financial and ethical implications.

Overall, the highest-paying jobs of the future will be those that blend technological proficiency with human judgement, leveraging our unique ability to think creatively, ethically, and strategically.

- *Space Pilot*

  The commercial space industry is getting 'ready to launch', so to speak. Which means that pilots who can fly a spacecraft will become a highly coveted job. As pilot jobs go, the most important qualification is logging in a specific number of hours in flight, but since we're talking about outer space, a background in astrophysics, astronomy, and engineering will also be necessary. As one would imagine, this is highly touted to be one of the highest paying jobs of the future.

- *Data Detective*

  Data usage is evolving, and so a data analyst's job needs to evolve along with it. By 2025, nearly 30 percent of data generated will be real-time, experts say. More than simple data processing and report generation, data information will also need to be translated into understandable, relatable terms so that those handling it can work to implement the necessary measures for improvement. Aside from the usual data analysing responsibilities, candidates for data detective jobs of the future 2025 also need to develop an investigative problem-solving mentality and practice an ability to demonstrate a keen understanding of data problems that need to be addressed.

- *Ethical Sourcing Manager*

Sourcing managers are responsible for handling an organisation's end-to-end sourcing functions, which includes finding the best suppliers, analysing and calculating procurement costs, and decreasing expenditure. As the world practices better environmental habits, sourcing managers will also have to be ethical with their approach to their job. Aside from ensuring that the sourced products are manufactured ethically, applicants for ethical sourcing manager jobs of the future also need to ensure that the entire sources of procurement follow ethical standards.

- *Extinct Species Revivalist*

Scientists estimate that between 200 and 2,000 species die off each year, with the dire effects of climate change expected to double the losses by 2040. Fortunately, the technology exists to revive extinct species—think Jurassic Park. From genome editing to extracting and synthesising DNA strands, extinct species revivalists will soon be able to recreate organisms and reintroduce them to their natural habitats. Extinct species revivalist jobs of the future 2040 require a strong understanding of biology, chemistry, and medicine, as well as a full understanding of geographical, ethical, and legal concerns that affect each revived species.

- *Companion for the Aged*

  By 2050, the number of people aged 60 years and over is projected to reach over 2 billion. As general life expectancy gets longer thanks to technology, ageing is expected to become one of the most important social concerns of the future. The job of companions for the aged will involve listening to them, helping them with their daily chores, and even taking them out for a stroll or some fresh air from time to time. Some of the key competencies necessary for this job of the future in 2050 include patience, empathy, and keen observation skills to see if the elderly person is experiencing any emotional problems, such as depression and anxiety.

- *IT Service Broker*

  With IT services in high demand, it becomes necessary for someone to play the role of negotiator between IT service providers and their customers. The growing adoption of IT means that the role of the IT service broker will only increase in importance. As someone who's ultimately responsible for intermediation, IT service brokers should be able to understand the customer's requirements and identify vendors who can meet them. Someone who has experience in real estate or stock brokering will find plenty of success in this field if they can shift their focus on IT, cloud computing, and other digital technologies.

- *AI Specialist*

  Candidates interested in pursuing opportunities for AI specialisation have a variety of routes to take—automation, robotics, computer programming, and other fields relating to maths, technology, logic, and engineering. There are also degree programmes that offer specific majors in AI or pursue an AI specialisation from within majors such as health informatics, engineering computer science, or information technology. As for the jobs themselves, AI specialists have a number of roles to fill, including research science, software engineering, algorithm programming, and AI consultancy.

- *UX Designer*

With interfaces becoming more and more prevalent, UX—short for user experience—will become the primary focus of customer satisfaction. UX Designers will be responsible for the complete appearance of products and websites, with the goal of delving into people's psyche and identifying their needs as consumers to help create a more enjoyable digital experience. Combining a background in graphic design and psychology will be helpful in progressing with this career trajectory.

- *3D Printing Engineer*

3D printing is a relatively new way of manufacturing that utilises computer-aided design (CAD). It requires high specialisation, and the best candidates for this job are those who have a serious interest in the process, organisation, and manufacturing, not to mention who take great pride in ensuring perfection in their work. An associate degree in a technical field, as well as proficiency in measuring tools, are essential requirements for this particular job of the future.

- *Digital Rehabilitation Counsellor*

People are only now realising how addictive and destructive social media and other online channels can be, with experts predicting it will be a major driver of mental health costs by 2030. Digital rehabilitation counsellors are tasked with helping people recover their digital overconsumption and regain their life back. As one of the most important jobs of the future 2030, becoming a digital rehabilitation counsellor requires a Bachelor's or Master's degree in counselling.

Is your resume ready for the jobs of the future? Do you have the skills it will take to fulfill these roles?

Some of these top-paying jobs of the future are already waiting to be filled today. To qualify and succeed in these jobs, you need to acquire the right skills, competencies, and mindset.

Part 4

JOB READINESS

*"Being literate, educated, and skilled are
three distinct pillars of personal empowerment."*

Transition From Campus to Corporate

"College life teaches the theory of success,
while corporate life demands its practice."

In the rapidly changing world of jobs in the era of Industry 4.0, job readiness has a whole new meaning and importance for fresh graduates. Various studies have discovered that nearly 87% of graduates globally are not considered job-ready. This percentage is higher in countries with large young populations, such as India, Indonesia, China, Bangladesh, Pakistan, Ethiopia, etc. Studies show that employers spend anywhere between three months to a year to make graduates job-ready or, in other words, fully productive. This job readiness does not include company or role-specific technical skills but other soft and life skills that are essential to function in the workplace.

The figure below illustrates a mapping of these skills expected by employers. These are not what universities are set up to deliver. Universities essentially are curriculum-driven and have little time, skill, or experience in inculcating these skills. If you wish to work overseas, then the demand for these skills goes up exponentially with the added expectation of cultural competence and adaptability to the country you are going to work in.

College life and corporate life are two very different stages of life. Here are some of the key philosophical differences:

- Freedom vs. responsibility: In college, you have a lot of freedom to do what you want, when you want. You can choose your classes, your extracurricular activities, and your social life. In corporate life, you have more responsibility. You are expected to meet deadlines, produce results, and work well with others.

- Structure vs. flexibility: College life is typically more structured than corporate life. You have classes to attend, assignments to complete, and exams to take. In corporate life, there is more flexibility. You may have a set schedule, but you may also have the freedom to work-from-home or set your own hours.

- Focus vs. distractions: In college, your focus is on your studies. You may have other commitments, such as work or extracurricular activities, but your studies are your top priority. In corporate life, you have to balance your work with other commitments, such as family, friends, and hobbies. There are also more distractions in the corporate world, such as email, social media, and meetings.

- Individual vs. team-oriented: In college, you are more likely to work on individual projects. In corporate life, you are more likely to work on team projects. This means that you need to be able to collaborate with others and share ideas.

- Learning vs. doing: In college, you learn the theory behind your chosen field. In corporate life, you apply that theory to real-world problems. This means that you need to be able to think critically and solve problems.

- Making the transition from college to corporate life can be a challenge, but it's also an exciting time. By understanding the key differences between these two stages of life, you can be prepared for the transition and make the most of your new career.

- In the absence of job readiness, most fresh graduates feel lost, frustrated, or inadequate at the workplace. They realise that their academic knowledge is only useful to a point. The real-world at work looks completely different. Here are some other very specific differences between campus life and corporate life that make the transition from campus to corporate difficult.

- At campus, you pay to learn, whereas at a corporate, you are paid to deliver a specified outcome. You are no longer a client of the university on a path of learning. You are now an adult who is expected to behave and deliver outputs as expected by the employer.

- At campus, you follow a defined path in the form of a curriculum. This has a certain predictability, certainty, and the comfort of having worked for others in the past attached to it. At the workplace, every situation is unique with consequences to either a client, shareholder, or fellow employee. You quickly realise that the campus academics had only 25 percent practicals, whereas the workplace is almost wholly an exercise in practicality.

- When you are at campus, you can decide which classes to take, which lecturers to skip based on your likes and dislikes, which day to go late or when to skip college altogether. At the workplace, even if working remotely and more so if you are an entrepreneur, you are expected to be on time every day, put in a certain number of hours, and work with everyone regardless of your likes and dislikes.

- When you are on campus, you can choose who to hang out with, who to study with, who to socialise or team up with. At work, there is no such choice. You must work with everyone regardless of likes, dislikes, race, gender, nationality, caste, creed, looks, personality, age, etc.

- At the campus and in schools, there is a trend to recognise and award people even if they do not succeed and come on top of their peers. Learners are given participation medals/certificates even if they come last. Imagine the shock of these learners when they go to work and realise coming second is considered to be a failure.

- Most academic courses are structured with an exam at the end of the semester or year. Chances are that you can read up past-year question papers and select key parts of the curriculum that have the highest chances of questions being asked, leaving out many topics of the curriculum. Even from the parts that you have studied, you probably have a choice of how many questions to answer from the total questions asked. In most cases, you need to attempt about 60-70 percent of the questions posed to you. From these questions posed to you, if you get sixty percent right or achieve a GPA of 3.0 and above, you are considered a good student. Pass marks are lower, around the 40 percent or 2.0 GPA point. At the workplace, any output delivered less than 100 percent accurate will lead to consequences.

- At the campus and throughout your academic life, you have worked individually. Studying on your own with sporadic help from others, preparing for tests and exams on your own, and the results reflect your progress. When you go to work for the first time, you are suddenly faced with the challenge of collaboration. For academics, how other students perform does not affect you. At the workplace, this is completely different as now you need to get information, work done, or other dependencies from a diverse set of people. You need to collaborate, work in a team, and still deliver. This is a new experience. The limited exposure to collaboration that you had in academic life was limited to some sports or cultural events, where you worked with your fellow students, people largely like you in age and youth culture.

- Dealing with authority, in the case of the workplace it is your boss, is another alien experience. Depending on how you were brought up and the kind of campus you spent time on, your initial shock may vary, but shocked you will be. When you are pursuing academics, the authority figures you deal with are generally your parents and your professors. Both have a benign and indulgent view of your struggles and failures. They motivate you and understand that you are still young, are learning, and will make mistakes. Any reprimand from them is easier to take and in some cases, we can even sulk if we feel we have been wrongly pulled up. Their position is also not threatened by your success. At the workplace, this is not so. Any error or mistake, whether wilful or out of ignorance, has consequences. Your boss will make their thoughts and displeasure known, sometimes publicly so. There is no room to sulk or avoid the boss. You have to go back to work and lift yourself up. There is unlikely to be an indulgent view or a motivational talk except in a few cases for the first-time mistake.

- High marks at the end of the semester or year in examinations define success in academic life. In a corporate setting, day-to-day consistent delivery at the least and excellence as a normal expectation define success. The degree of competitiveness among peers in the workplace to advance in their careers is nothing compared to the competitiveness on campus to achieve higher marks.

What can you, as a fresh graduate or an early career professional, do to make this transition easier? For this, let us first look at what employers expect as employability skills and how you can develop them.

Navigating the Future: Top Employability Skills for Fresh Graduates

"Mastering today's skills paves the way for tomorrow's success, transforming potential into prosperity."

In a fluid job market, fresh graduates face the daunting challenge of standing out among a sea of qualified candidates. As technology advances and the global economy shifts, the skills required to not only land a job but excel in one's career are also changing. This chapter delves into the critical employability skills that fresh graduates need to cultivate to ensure their success in the future workplace. Some of these have been explained earlier in the book. There is an element of repetition, but this section looks at the same skills from the perspective of a fresh graduate.

1. Digital Literacy

In the digital age, proficiency with technology is not just preferred; it's expected. Digital literacy goes beyond basic computer skills to include understanding and leveraging digital tools and platforms, from cloud-based software to data analysis tools, and even emerging technologies like artificial intelligence (AI) and blockchain. Graduates who can navigate digital tools efficiently, adapt to new technologies, and understand the digital ecosystem will be highly valued.

2. Critical Thinking and Problem-Solving

The ability to think critically and solve complex problems is invaluable in any role. Employers are looking for individuals who can analyse situations, think creatively, and develop innovative solutions to challenges. This involves not just technical skills but also the ability to question assumptions, interpret data, and apply knowledge in practical, effective ways.

3. Communication Skills

Effective communication is crucial in the workplace, encompassing both verbal and writing skills. This includes the ability to clearly convey ideas, listen actively, and engage in constructive dialogue. In a globalised world, communication also extends to intercultural competence—the ability to communicate effectively with people from diverse backgrounds and cultures.

4. Emotional Intelligence (EI)

Emotional intelligence—the capacity to be aware of, control, and express one's emotions, and to handle interpersonal relationships judiciously and empathetically—is increasingly recognised as a pivotal skill. High EI enables individuals to navigate workplace dynamics, collaborate effectively, and lead with empathy, fostering a positive, productive work environment.

5. Adaptability and Flexibility

The only constant in the job market is change. As industries evolve, the ability to adapt and remain flexible is key. This means being open to learning new skills, embracing change, and being willing to pivot roles or responsibilities as needed. Adaptive individuals can thrive in dynamic environments, making them invaluable assets to any organisation.

6. Leadership and Teamwork

Leadership is not just for managers. Employers value the ability to take initiative, motivate peers, and contribute positively to team dynamics. This includes being a collaborative team player, having a strong sense of accountability, and the capacity to lead projects or groups effectively, even in non-managerial roles.

7. Continuous Learning

The commitment to lifelong learning is essential in a world where new knowledge and skills are constantly required. Fresh graduates should demonstrate a willingness to learn, upskill, and reskill throughout their careers. This proactive approach to personal and professional development can set individuals apart in a competitive job market.

8. Entrepreneurial Mindset

An entrepreneurial mindset—characterised by innovation, risk-taking, and resilience—is valuable even for those not starting a business. This skill set encourages thinking outside the box, identifying opportunities for improvement, and persisting in the face of setbacks. It reflects an individual's ability to drive change and innovation within their role or organisation.

As we look to the future, the landscape of employability skills is both broadening and deepening. Fresh graduates must equip themselves with a diverse set of skills that blend technical proficiency with soft skills like communication, emotional intelligence, and critical thinking. By fostering these competencies, graduates can not only secure their foothold in the job market but also pave the way for a successful and fulfilling career. The journey from academia to the professional world is a transition that demands adaptability, continuous learning, and an open-minded approach to challenges and opportunities alike.

Digital Literacy

"Being digitally illiterate today is akin to being unable to read and write in the past; both leave individuals disconnected from the core of societal progress."

The rapid evolution of technology and its integration into virtually every aspect of daily life and work has made digital literacy an indispensable skill for fresh graduates entering the workforce. This goes beyond the basic ability to navigate social media or use a word processor; it encompasses a broad set of competencies that include understanding and utilising digital tools, platforms, and services effectively, securely, and creatively to solve problems, communicate, and manage information. Here's an exploration of why digital literacy is crucial for fresh graduates, supported by real-life examples.

1. Navigating the Modern Workplace

The modern workplace is increasingly digital, with tools and platforms for collaboration (like Slack, Microsoft Teams), project management (such as Asana, Trello), and remote work becoming standard. For instance, during the COVID-19 pandemic, companies worldwide shifted to remote work, a trend that has persisted. This shift demonstrated the importance of being able to use digital communication tools effectively, not just for basic tasks but for engaging in complex collaborative projects. Fresh graduates with a high level of digital literacy can adapt more quickly to these environments, leveraging technology to stay productive and connected, regardless of physical location.

2. Data Literacy

With the advent of big data, the ability to understand and analyse data has become a key skill in many industries. This includes not only interpreting data sets but also understanding how to use data analytics tools and software. For example, marketing professionals now rely heavily on data analytics to gauge campaign success and customer preferences. A graduate who can use Google Analytics to derive insights about user behaviour on a website provides immediate value to employers, demonstrating the practical importance of digital literacy in making informed business decisions.

3. Cybersecurity Awareness

The increase in cyber threats has made cybersecurity knowledge essential. Digital literacy now involves understanding the basics of internet safety, secure password practices, and the ability to recognise phishing attempts and other forms of cyber attacks. An example of this in practice is an employee being able to identify and report a suspicious email, thereby preventing a potential data breach. Fresh graduates who are aware of these risks and know-how to navigate them safely can protect themselves and their employers from significant losses.

4. Continuous Learning and Adaptability

The technological landscape is constantly changing, with new tools and technologies emerging at a rapid pace. Digital literacy includes the ability to learn and adapt to new digital tools and platforms efficiently. A real-life example of this is the transition from traditional office software to cloud-based collaboration tools like Google Workspace or Microsoft 365. Graduates who can quickly learn and master these new tools can keep pace with changing workplace demands, making them more valuable and versatile employees.

5. Innovation and Problem-Solving

Digital literacy fosters an environment of innovation and creativity. For example, knowledge of digital fabrication tools like 3D printers and laser cutters enables engineers and designers to prototype new products quickly and cost-effectively. Similarly, familiarity with coding and software development can open up opportunities for creating custom solutions to business problems. A graduate who can automate a time-consuming data entry process through a simple script not only demonstrates digital literacy but also significantly contributes to operational efficiency.

Digital literacy is no longer a supplementary skill but a fundamental requirement for success in the modern workforce. It enables fresh graduates to navigate the digital workplace, leverage data for insights, ensure cybersecurity, continuously learn and adapt to new technologies, and innovate. As technology continues to evolve, the depth and breadth of digital literacy required will only increase, making it an essential component of education and professional development for all aspiring professionals.

Critical Thinking and Problem-Solving

"Critical thinking illuminates the path, while problem solving paves the way, together forging a route to innovation and understanding."

Critical thinking and problem-solving are intertwined skills that enable individuals to analyse information, identify problems, evaluate alternatives, and implement solutions effectively. Critical thinking involves questioning assumptions, analysing perspectives, and evaluating the validity of arguments or solutions. Problem-solving, on the other hand, is the application of critical thinking to overcome challenges and achieve goals.

Real-Life Applications

Innovative Solutions to Environmental Challenges: Consider the case of young entrepreneurs who developed a biodegradable alternative to plastic straws made from seaweed. This innovation required critical thinking to identify the environmental impact of plastic as a significant problem and problem-solving to design and test a sustainable solution. Their approach not only offers an eco-friendly alternative but also opens pathways for addressing broader issues of plastic pollution.

Healthcare Breakthroughs Through Critical Analysis: In the healthcare sector, a group of graduate researchers used critical thinking to question the efficacy of traditional treatment protocols for a rare disease. By analysing patient data and existing studies, they identified a potential for improvement and developed a novel treatment approach. Their problem-solving skills were crucial in designing the clinical trials, which eventually led to a more effective treatment method, showcasing how critical thinking can lead to significant advancements in patient care.

Technology and Cybersecurity: With the rise of cyber threats, a team of computer science graduates applied their critical thinking skills to analyse vulnerability in existing cybersecurity measures. Through rigorous problem-solving, they developed an innovative encryption algorithm that significantly enhanced data security for a major tech company. This example highlights the importance of these skills in addressing and mitigating the ever-evolving cyber threats in the digital age.

Why These Skills Matter Now More Than Ever

Adaptability in a Changing Job Market: As automation and AI transform industries, the ability to think critically and solve complex problems ensures that graduates can adapt to new roles that machines cannot easily replicate.

Global Challenges: From climate change to global pandemics, the world faces unprecedented challenges that require innovative solutions. Graduates equipped with these skills are better prepared to contribute to solving these complex global issues.

Innovation and Economic Growth: Economies thrive on innovation, which is spurred by individuals who can think critically about problems and develop creative solutions. Graduates who can do this drive progress and competitiveness in the global market.

The demand for critical thinking and problem-solving skills among fresh graduates is a reflection of our times. These skills are the bedrock upon which the future workforce will navigate uncertainty, drive innovation, and address the multifaceted challenges of our world. Real-life examples from environmental innovation, healthcare breakthroughs, and cybersecurity advancements illustrate the profound impact of these skills. As educators, policymakers, and industry leaders, the onus is on us to cultivate these abilities in the next generation, ensuring they are well-equipped to lead us into a promising future.

In today's dynamic job market, the ability to effectively communicate and connect with others—termed as communication and interpersonal skills—stands as a cornerstone for career readiness, especially for recent graduates. This comprehensive skill set transcends mere linguistic proficiency, embodying the ability to navigate a globally interconnected and culturally diverse workspace. Here's an in-depth look into why these skills are pivotal and how one can cultivate them through real-life strategies.

Global Workplace Dynamics

The modern workplace, reshaped by the post-pandemic era, often involves collaboration with colleagues from varied nationalities, cultures, and backgrounds. The rise of remote work has further diversified team compositions across gender, age, and geography. English, serving as the lingua franca in many global settings, necessitates not only fluency in spoken forms but also a command of business English. To enhance language skills, engaging with English media—such as BBC news broadcasts, newspapers, and films—can be beneficial. Additionally, choosing English as a college elective or enrolling in language courses can provide structured learning opportunities.

Clear and Precise Communication

The essence of effective workplace communication lies in the ability to articulate thoughts, ideas, and feedback clearly and concisely, ensuring comprehensibility across diverse cultural and linguistic backgrounds. This skill can be honed through academic assignments, participation in debates, group projects, and the organisation of campus events. Writing about current events, even for personal growth, can sharpen one's ability to express complex ideas succinctly.

Active Listening and Empathy

Understanding and being understood is a two-way street; active listening is as critical as speaking. It involves fully engaging with the speaker, asking insightful questions, and showing empathy. This can be practiced in everyday conversations by being present, avoiding premature judgements, and seeking clarity through open-ended questions. Empathy, demonstrated through verbal affirmations and sharing relevant personal experiences, fosters a supportive dialogue environment.

Presentation and Public Speaking

Confidence in public speaking and presentation is invaluable, offering a platform to showcase one's ideas and leadership.

Campus debates, project presentations, and involvement in student organisations offer a safe and supportive environment to develop these skills.

Real-life Examples

Global Team Collaboration: Consider a project manager coordinating a team across the US, India, and Germany. The ability to communicate effectively, considering cultural nuances and varying English proficiency levels, ensures project success and team harmony.

Active Listening in Client Meetings: A consultant uses active listening techniques to fully understand a client's needs, asking open-ended questions to delve deeper into the client's concerns, thereby building trust and delivering tailored solutions.

Public Speaking Success: A recent graduate presents their startup idea at a local business competition, using clear, persuasive language and engaging storytelling to capture the audience's attention and win funding.

Mastering communication and interpersonal skills is not just about excelling in the language but about understanding and connecting with people from diverse backgrounds. By actively engaging in opportunities to speak, listen, and empathise, fresh graduates can significantly enhance their employability and pave the way for successful careers in a globally connected world.

Emotional Intelligence

"Emotional intelligence is the anchor that keeps us grounded amid the waves of change and uncertainty."

In today's rapidly evolving job market, the importance of technical skills cannot be overstated. However, an often-overlooked asset that is equally crucial for fresh graduates entering the workforce is emotional intelligence (EI). Emotional intelligence, the ability to recognise, understand, manage, and use emotions effectively, not only enhances personal wellbeing but also significantly impacts one's professional success. It is the cornerstone of building strong interpersonal relationships, navigating workplace challenges, and leading with compassion and insight.

At the heart of EI is self-awareness. Understanding one's emotions serves as a foundation for empathy, decision-making, and stress management, essential components for thriving in any career. For instance, consider Sarah, a recent graduate who joined a marketing firm. Sarah quickly realised that her ability to identify her emotions and manage stress was crucial during high-pressure campaigns. Her capacity to remain composed and make clear-headed decisions under stress not only improved her performance but also positively influenced her team's morale and productivity.

Another critical aspect of emotional intelligence is self-regulation. This skill is about controlling one's emotions and adapting to changing circumstances. James, a junior developer, demonstrated this when he received constructive criticism on his project. Instead of reacting defensively, he assessed his emotions, recognised the opportunity for growth, and responded with gratitude. This approach not only facilitated his professional development but also strengthened his relationships with colleagues, showcasing the profound impact of emotional regulation in a professional setting.

Empathy, the ability to understand and share the feelings of another, is a cornerstone of EI that fosters effective teamwork and leadership. Emily, a project manager, exemplified this when she noticed a team member struggling with personal issues. By offering support and adjusting project timelines, she not only helped her colleague through a difficult time but also ensured the project's success. Her empathetic leadership enhanced team cohesion and loyalty, illustrating how empathy can lead to better outcomes for individuals and organisations alike.

Moreover, emotional intelligence is indispensable for effective communication and conflict resolution. For example, Alex, a customer service representative, used his high EI to de-escalate a heated conversation with a dissatisfied customer. By acknowledging the customer's emotions and demonstrating understanding, Alex transformed a potentially damaging interaction into a positive experience, retaining the customer and enhancing the company's reputation.

Furthermore, in the context of leadership, EI is invaluable. Leaders like Sofia, who led with emotional intelligence, create an environment of trust and respect. Sofia's ability to sense team dynamics and address unspoken concerns has made her an admired leader. Her empathetic approach to leadership has not only boosted team performance but also fostered a culture of innovation and inclusivity.

As the workplace continues to evolve, the demand for professionals who possess not only technical skills but also a high degree of emotional intelligence will rise. Emotional intelligence empowers individuals to excel in their roles, navigate the complexities of interpersonal relationships, lead with empathy, and create positive, resilient organisations. For fresh graduates stepping into their careers, developing emotional intelligence is not just an option but a necessity for achieving lasting success and fulfilment in the professional world.

Adaptability and Flexibility

*"Embrace adaptability and flexibility in your career choices,
for the path to success is rarely a straight line, but a
dynamic journey of growth and discovery."*

The capacity for adaptability and flexibility stands out as a critical determinant of success, especially for fresh graduates stepping into their careers. This chapter delves into the importance of these traits, underlining how they can serve as the bedrock for not only surviving but thriving in the fluctuating job market of today.

Adaptability refers to an individual's ability to adjust to changes and new conditions efficiently. It encompasses a willingness to learn new skills, embrace new technologies, and adapt to new roles and environments. Flexibility, on the other hand, is the ability to be versatile and willing to alter plans or directions in response to changing circumstances. Together, these qualities ensure that fresh graduates can navigate the complexities and uncertainties inherent in modern work environments.

The relevance of adaptability and flexibility has been magnified by the rapid pace of technological advancement and the shifting economic landscape. Industries today are in a constant state of flux, with new roles being created as quickly as old ones become obsolete. For instance, the rise of artificial intelligence and automation has transformed numerous professions, necessitating a workforce that is not only tech-savvy but also capable of continuously acquiring new competencies.

Real-life Examples at the Workplace

Embracing Digital Transformation

Consider the case of a marketing professional who began their career focused on traditional advertising mediums. As digital marketing's prominence grew, those who adapted by learning about SEO, social media advertising, and content marketing found new opportunities. In contrast, those who resisted change found themselves at a disadvantage. Adaptability in learning new digital tools and strategies became a key differentiator in their career progression.

Pivoting Roles Amidst Organisational Changes

Another example is that of an employee in a tech company who started as a software developer. When the company decided to pivot its product strategy based on market feedback, this individual took the initiative to learn about product management and user experience design. Their flexibility in taking on new responsibilities allowed them to transition into a role that was crucial for the company's new direction, thereby securing their position and contributing significantly to the project's success.

Adjusting to Remote Work

The COVID-19 pandemic serves as a stark example of the need for adaptability. Companies and employees worldwide had to transition to remote work almost overnight. Those fresh graduates who quickly adapted to this new mode of working, by setting up effective home offices, mastering communication and collaboration tools, and finding ways to maintain productivity, demonstrated their value. Their ability to remain flexible under such unprecedented conditions highlighted their potential for leadership and resilience.

For fresh graduates, cultivating adaptability and flexibility is not just about enhancing their employability. It's about preparing for a career that will inevitably involve transitions, challenges, and opportunities that we cannot yet foresee. By embracing these qualities, graduates equip themselves with a mindset geared towards continuous learning and growth. This not only benefits their personal career trajectories but also makes them invaluable contributors to any organisation, capable of leading change rather than being led by it.

In essence, the adaptability and flexibility of fresh graduates are the catalysts for innovation and progress within the workplace. They are the skills that will allow individuals to not just navigate but excel in the future job market, no matter how it evolves.

Leadership and Teamwork

"True leadership in young graduates shines through teamwork, as one without the other is an incomplete path to success."

In the modern workplace, the significance of leadership and teamwork extends far beyond traditional managerial roles. For fresh graduates stepping into their first jobs, these skills are not just advantageous but essential for career success and growth. Leadership, often misconceived as a skill reserved for those in executive positions, is increasingly recognised for its value at every level within organisations. Teamwork, similarly, is not just about getting along with colleagues but about harnessing collective strengths to achieve common goals.

Leadership: Not Just for Managers

Leadership is about influence, not authority. It involves inspiring and motivating those around you to achieve shared objectives. For fresh graduates, demonstrating leadership can mean taking initiative in projects, offering innovative solutions to problems, or stepping forward to coordinate team efforts in times of uncertainty. This proactive approach is highly valued by employers, as it contributes significantly to the team's and the organisation's overall success.

Real-life example: Consider the story of Sarah, a recent graduate who joined a marketing team at a mid-sized firm. Despite being the newest member, Sarah noticed a gap in the team's social media strategy. Instead of waiting for her superiors to address the issue, she took the initiative to research and propose a new approach that significantly increased engagement rates. Sarah's ability to identify a problem, take charge, and implement a solution showcased her leadership potential, earning her recognition and a promotion within her first year.

Teamwork: A Collective Strength

Teamwork is about combining the unique skills, experiences, and perspectives of each team member to achieve a common goal. It requires communication, respect, and a willingness to collaborate closely with others, even under pressure. For fresh graduates, being a collaborative team player means actively listening to others, contributing ideas, and being adaptable to changing roles or responsibilities within the team.

Real-life example: Alex, a recent engineering graduate, joined a project team tasked with developing a new product. The project faced numerous challenges, including tight deadlines and technical difficulties. Alex's ability to work closely with his teammates, leveraging his technical skills while benefiting from the experience of more senior colleagues, was crucial. Together, the team managed to overcome obstacles and deliver the project on time. Alex's willingness to learn from others and contribute his expertise exemplified the power of effective teamwork.

The Synergy of Leadership and Teamwork

Leadership and teamwork are interdependent. Effective leaders are those who can unite a team, steering it towards success, while a cohesive team often empowers individual members to emerge as leaders in their own right. This synergy is crucial for fresh graduates to understand and embrace. By developing both leadership and teamwork skills, they can contribute more effectively to their organisations, drive innovation, and navigate the complexities of the modern workplace.

Real-life example: Maya, a fresh graduate in a technology startup, found herself leading a small team on a pilot project. Her ability to listen, incorporate feedback, and motivate her team not only led to the project's success but also fostered a culture of mutual respect and collaboration. Maya's story illustrates how leadership intertwined with effective teamwork can create an environment where innovation thrives, and objectives are met more efficiently.

For fresh graduates, mastering the art of leadership and teamwork is not optional but a necessity for success in today's dynamic job market. By taking initiative, being proactive in problem-solving, and fostering a spirit of collaboration, they can make a significant impact from the outset of their careers. These skills enable them to navigate workplace challenges, contribute to their organisations' growth, and pave the way for their own professional development. The stories of Sarah, Alex, and Maya serve as inspiring examples of how leadership and teamwork can transform fresh graduates into invaluable assets for any organisation.

Continuous Learning

"Curiosity is the spark that ignites the flame of lifelong learning, transforming every moment into an opportunity for discovery."

The mantra for success for fresh graduates is no longer just about having a degree or specific skill set but about embracing continuous learning. The acceleration of technological advancements and shifts in workplace dynamics demand a workforce that is adaptable, flexible, and perpetually willing to learn. This chapter delves into why continuous learning is paramount for fresh graduates and how it can be a pivotal factor in their long-term career success.

Understanding the Landscape

The world we live in is changing at an unprecedented pace. Industries that once thrived are now evolving or disappearing, replaced by new sectors and technologies. For instance, the rise of artificial intelligence, renewable energy, and digital marketing are reshaping the job market. This transformation requires fresh graduates to not only enter the workforce with a solid foundation but also to continue building upon it. The commitment to lifelong learning becomes not just beneficial but essential.

Real-Life Importance of Continuous Learning

Continuous learning in the workplace can take many forms, from formal education such as workshops and online courses to more informal methods like self-study, peer learning, and on-the-job training. Here are real-life examples demonstrating its importance:

Adapting to Technological Advances: Consider the case of a marketing graduate entering the workforce. With the digital landscape constantly evolving, skills in social media, analytics, and digital advertising become outdated quickly. Continuous learning allows this individual to stay ahead of the curve, mastering new platforms and tools as they emerge, thereby making them invaluable to their employer.

Career Progression: Sarah, an engineer at a renewable energy firm, realised that to advance in her career, she needed to understand project management and the economics of renewable energy projects. By pursuing relevant certifications and courses, she not only expanded her skill set but also positioned herself for leadership roles, illustrating how continuous learning can lead to career growth.

Navigating Career Shifts: John, after working in sales for a decade, found his passion for data science. Through online courses and self-study, he acquired the necessary skills to make a successful career transition. His story highlights how continuous learning can facilitate a seamless shift into new, in-demand fields.

Building a Culture of Learning

For fresh graduates, cultivating a habit of continuous learning begins with a mindset shift. Viewing learning as an ongoing journey rather than a destination can transform how they approach their careers. Employers play a crucial role in this by fostering a learning culture, offering opportunities for development, and encouraging exploration.

The importance of continuous learning for fresh graduates cannot be overstated. It is a critical driver for personal development, career advancement, and adaptability in the face of change. By committing to lifelong learning, individuals not only enhance their employability but also pave the way for fulfilling and dynamic careers. As the landscape of work continues to evolve, the willingness to learn, upskill, and reskill will set apart the leaders of tomorrow from the rest. Fresh graduates must, therefore, embrace continuous learning as not just a strategy for success but as a way of life.

Entrepreneurial Mindset

"An entrepreneurial mindset isn't confined to starting a business; it's about transforming challenges into opportunities, driving innovation, and continuously learning to excel in any career path."

In today's job market, fresh graduates are navigating an increasingly competitive and uncertain landscape. The traditional path of climbing the corporate ladder has given way to a more dynamic environment, where innovation, adaptability, and resilience are key. It's within this context that an entrepreneurial mindset emerges as an invaluable asset for those entering the workforce. This mindset, characterised by innovation, risk-taking, and resilience, is not only crucial for those aspiring to start their own ventures but equally vital for individuals seeking to excel in their careers within organisations.

The Essence of an Entrepreneurial Mindset

An entrepreneurial mindset is about more than just business acumen or the desire to launch a startup. It embodies a way of thinking that enables individuals to identify opportunities, overcome challenges, and drive change. It encourages fresh graduates to think outside the box, embrace risk as an opportunity for learning, and persist in the face of setbacks. This mindset is about seeing the bigger picture and leveraging creativity to solve problems and create value.

Real-Life Workplace Applications

Innovation in Action: Consider the story of Maya, a junior marketing analyst at a mid-sized tech firm. Faced with declining engagement rates on the company's social media platforms, Maya proposed a bold new content strategy centred around interactive, user-generated content. Despite initial scepticism, her willingness to experiment and her data-driven approach led to a significant uptick in engagement and user retention. Maya's story highlights how an entrepreneurial mindset can drive innovation within an organisation, turning challenges into opportunities for growth.

Risk-Taking and Learning: Alex, a recent graduate, joined a startup as a product developer. When tasked with leading a project to develop a new software feature, Alex encountered numerous setbacks, including technical glitches and shifting user requirements. However, instead of being deterred by these challenges, Alex viewed them as a chance to learn and iterate. His persistence and willingness to take calculated risks eventually resulted in a successful product launch. Alex's experience underscores the importance of resilience and learning from failure, key components of an entrepreneurial mindset.

Driving Change with Resilience: Sarah, an entry-level engineer in a traditional manufacturing company, noticed inefficiencies in the production process that were leading to wasted resources and increased costs. Despite initial resistance from her team, Sarah persisted, conducting her own research and presenting a compelling case for adopting lean manufacturing principles. Her resilience and proactive approach not only led to significant cost savings but also positioned her as a change agent within the company.

Cultivating an Entrepreneurial Mindset

For fresh graduates looking to cultivate an entrepreneurial mindset, the journey begins with embracing a mindset of continuous learning and curiosity. Seeking out challenges, being open to feedback, and learning from both successes and failures are crucial. Networking with mentors and peers who embody this mindset can provide valuable insights and inspiration.

Additionally, developing skills in critical thinking, problem-solving, and effective communication can enhance one's ability to identify opportunities and drive change. Pursuing projects outside one's comfort zone, whether within a job role or through extracurricular activities, can also foster the kind of innovative thinking and resilience that characterises an entrepreneurial mindset.

An entrepreneurial mindset is not just for entrepreneurs. It's a transformative approach to professional development and career advancement. By cultivating this mindset, fresh graduates equip themselves with the tools to navigate the complexities of the modern workforce, drive innovation within their roles, and carve out a path to success that is both fulfilling and impactful. Embracing this mindset is about preparing for a future where adaptability, creative problem-solving, and resilience are not just desired but essential.

Navigating the Transition from Campus to Corporate

"Transitioning from academia to the corporate world is not just a career move; it's a journey of self-discovery, growth, and transformation."

The journey from the academic world to the corporate sector is an exciting yet challenging adventure, marking a significant milestone in one's career. As you stand on the brink of this monumental shift, it's essential to understand that while the transition may seem daunting, it is also filled with opportunities for growth, learning, and professional development. This chapter aims to guide you through this journey, offering actionable advice and strategies to ensure a smooth and successful transition.

Early Networking: The Foundation of Your Career

The importance of networking cannot be overstated in the context of transitioning from campus to corporate. Networking is not merely a job search tactic; it is a career development strategy that opens doors to opportunities, insights, and mentorships that are otherwise inaccessible. Begin by connecting with alumni, attending industry conferences, and participating in professional associations related to your field. These connections can provide valuable advice, introduce you to potential employers, and help you understand the nuances of your industry.

Mastery of Communication and Interpersonal Skills

In the corporate world, your ability to communicate effectively and navigate interpersonal dynamics can set you apart. This encompasses more than just the ability to speak and write clearly; it involves active listening, empathy, and the ability to work collaboratively with colleagues from diverse backgrounds. Embrace opportunities to refine these skills through group projects, presentations, and campus leadership roles. These experiences are invaluable, preparing you to engage confidently and constructively in professional settings.

Cultivating a Strong Work Ethic and Positive Attitude

Employers value individuals who demonstrate a strong work ethic and a positive, can-do attitude. This means showing initiative, being reliable, and consistently striving for excellence in your work. It also means approaching challenges with optimism and resilience. Cultivate these traits by embracing responsibilities, seeking constructive feedback, and viewing setbacks as opportunities for growth.

Effective Time Management and Prioritisation

The ability to manage your time effectively and prioritise tasks is critical in the fast-paced corporate environment. Develop these skills by setting clear goals, organising your tasks, and using tools or methods that enhance productivity. Learning to distinguish between urgent and important tasks will help you focus on priorities and deliver results efficiently.

Gaining Practical Experience

Practical experience, whether through internships, part-time jobs, or volunteer work, is invaluable. These opportunities not only bolster your resume but also provide a glimpse into the workings of industries and roles, helping you make informed career choices. Seek experiences that align with your interests and career goals, and approach them with a mindset of learning and contribution.

Learning, Adaptability, and the Willingness to Seek Help

The corporate landscape is ever-evolving, necessitating a commitment to continuous learning and adaptability. Be proactive in seeking knowledge, embracing new technologies, and adapting to changes in your industry. Moreover, don't hesitate to seek guidance when needed. Leveraging the expertise and experience of mentors and colleagues can accelerate your learning and integration into the corporate culture.

Professionalism in Conduct and Appearance

Understanding and aligning with the professional norms of your industry, including dress code and punctuality, is crucial. These aspects of professionalism convey your respect for the organisation and your role within it. Being punctual, dressing appropriately, and maintaining a professional demeanour in interactions demonstrate your commitment and respect for your colleagues and the corporate ethos.

Embracing Feedback and Teamwork

Feedback is a powerful tool for professional development. Approach it with an open mind, viewing it as an opportunity to improve and excel. Similarly, teamwork is at the heart of corporate success. Being a supportive and collaborative team member not only enhances your work environment but also contributes to collective achievements.

Transitioning from campus to corporate is a journey of transformation that requires preparation, adaptability, and a positive outlook. By networking early, honing your professional skills, and embracing the values of teamwork and continuous learning, you can navigate this transition successfully. Remember, this transition is not just about finding a job; it's about laying the groundwork for a fulfilling career. Embrace this journey with enthusiasm and openness, and you will find that the corporate world offers a landscape rich with opportunities for growth and success.

Navigating the Job Market as a Fresh Graduate

"At University you paid to get lessons;
at work you are paid to implement the lessons error free."

In the journey from academia to the professional world, fresh graduates often find themselves at the threshold of countless possibilities yet surrounded by intense competition and high expectations. Preparing for a job search is not just about landing any job; it's about setting the foundation for a fulfilling career. This chapter aims to guide you through the essential steps to ensure you are job-ready, leveraging your unique skills and aspirations to carve out a successful path in your chosen field.

Defining Your Career Goals

Embarking on your job search without clear career goals is like setting sail without a compass. Start by introspecting about what you truly desire from your career. Consider your interests, skills, and values. What industries fascinate you? What job roles ignite your passion? By answering these questions, you can chart a course that aligns with your aspirations, making your job search more focused and your career more rewarding.

Understanding Your Industry and Desired Roles

Knowledge is power, especially when it comes to understanding the landscape of your chosen industry and the roles within it. Dive deep into research to grasp the nuances of various job roles, the skills and qualifications they require, and the trends shaping the industry. This knowledge not only helps you tailor your applications but also prepares you for meaningful conversations during networking and interviews.

Crafting Your Professional Narrative

Your resume and cover letter are your ambassadors in the job market. They should not only list your qualifications and experiences but also tell a compelling story of your potential. Highlight relevant coursework, internships, and part-time jobs, and draw attention to any projects or achievements that showcase your skills. Remember, customisation is key—adapt your narrative for each application to underline your suitability for the role.

Building an Online Presence

In today's digital age, your online persona can be as crucial as your real-world interactions. A professional LinkedIn profile serves as your digital resume and a platform for networking. Connect with industry professionals, engage with relevant content, and contribute your insights to establish yourself as a knowledgeable and passionate candidate.

Networking: Your Gateway to Opportunities

Networking is an invaluable tool in your job search arsenal. It can open doors to opportunities that are not publicly advertised and provide insights into your industry and job market. Leverage both your personal and professional networks, attend career fairs, and participate in industry events. Remember, networking is about building genuine relationships rather than just collecting contacts.

Gaining Practical Experience

In a market where experience is often a prerequisite, internships, apprenticeships, and volunteer work are golden opportunities to build your resume. These experiences not only enhance your skills but also demonstrate your commitment and passion to potential employers. Seek out opportunities that align with your career goals and make the most of them.

Upskilling and Staying Updated

The only constant in any industry is change. Stay ahead of the curve by continuously enhancing your skills and acquiring relevant certifications. Whether it's through online courses, workshops, or further education, investing in your professional development shows employers your dedication to your career and your adaptability to industry shifts.

Mastering the Interview

Interviews can be daunting, but preparation is the key to confidence. Familiarise yourself with common interview questions and practice articulating your thoughts. Mock interviews with friends or mentors can provide valuable feedback and help hone your communication skills. Remember, an interview is also your opportunity to assess the fit between you and the employer.

The Proactive Job Search

The job market waits for no one. Be proactive in your search by exploring various channels such as online job boards, company websites, and professional networks. Customise your applications and don't hesitate to follow up. Each application is a step closer to your goal.

Embracing Positivity and Persistence

Job searching is a marathon, not a sprint. It's crucial to maintain a positive outlook and resilience in the face of challenges. Embrace feedback, refine your strategies, and continue to pursue your goals with determination.

Transitioning from a fresh graduate to a valued professional is a journey laden with challenges and opportunities. By defining clear career goals, understanding your industry, crafting a compelling professional narrative, and embracing continuous learning and networking, you are setting the stage for a successful career. Remember, job readiness is not a destination but a continuous journey of growth and improvement. Stay motivated, adaptable, and persistent, and the right opportunities will come your way.

Mastering the Art of Resume-Writing for Fresh Graduates

"Crafting an effective resume is the master key that unlocks the corporate door, turning opportunities into realities."

In the journey from academia to the professional world, your resume stands as a pivotal tool in bridging the gap. It's not just a document; it's a testament to your achievements, skills, and potential. For fresh graduates, crafting a resume that stands out in a sea of applicants is crucial. This chapter delves into the nuances of resume-writing, emphasising the power of strategic word choice and offering actionable insights to elevate your resume from good to exceptional.

The Power of Action Verbs in Leadership

In the realm of resume-writing, the distinction often lies in the details. Among these, the choice of words plays a paramount role. Specifically, action verbs that convey leadership are invaluable. Words like "Achieved," "Managed," and "Transformed" are not just verbs; they are narratives of your capability to lead, innovate, and excel.

Research underscores the impact of these power words. A study by The Ladders found that recruiters spend an average of 6 seconds on an initial resume scan. Within this brief window, action verbs capture attention, conveying your achievements and leadership prowess succinctly and memorably.

Crafting Your Leadership Story

Utilising leadership-oriented action verbs is the first step. The next is to weave these into compelling narratives of your professional experiences. For instance:

Achieved: Highlight quantifiable accomplishments, such as "Achieved a 20% increase in customer satisfaction by implementing a new feedback system."

Managed: Detail your leadership scope, "Managed a team of 15, directing project workflows and deadlines to enhance productivity by 30%."

Transformed: Show how your initiative led to significant changes, "Transformed the company's digital marketing strategy, resulting in a 40% increase in online engagement."

Advocated: "Advocated for the needs of my team members and ensured that they had the resources they needed to be successful."

Appointed: "Appointed as team leader and responsible for the day-to-day operations of the team."

Coached: "Coached and mentored new employees on the company's policies and procedures."

Collaborated: "Collaborated with cross-functional teams to develop and implement new marketing campaigns."

Communicated: "Communicated effectively with both internal and external stakeholders to ensure that everyone was on the same page."

Delegated: "Delegated tasks to team members and ensured that they were completed on time and to the highest standards."

Directed: "Directed a team of 20 employees and oversaw the day-to-day operations of the department."

Empowered: "Empowered team members to take ownership of their projects and make decisions."

Envisioned: "Envisioned a new marketing campaign that resulted in a 20% increase in website traffic."

Established: "Established a new training programme for new employees that resulted in a 90% reduction in employee turnover."

Facilitated: "Facilitated a meeting of fifty stakeholders and ensured that the meeting was productive."

Generated: "Generated £1 million in new sales by developing and executing a new marketing campaign."

Influenced: "Influenced senior management to approve a new product development project."

Instructed: "Instructed a team of ten employees on the use of new software."

Launched: "Launched a new product that resulted in a 10% increase in sales."

Motivated: "Motivated a team of employees to achieve their goals."

Oversaw: "Oversaw the day-to-day operations of the department and ensured that all projects were completed on time and to the highest standards."

Pioneered: "Pioneered a new marketing strategy that resulted in a 30% increase in website traffic."

Reorganised: "Reorganised the department and resulted in a 15% increase in efficiency."

Spearheaded: "Spearheaded a new product development project that resulted in £1 million in new sales."

Streamlined: "Streamlined the company's internal processes and resulted in a 10% reduction in costs."

Won: "Won a national award for outstanding leadership."

Each example pairs an action verb with a quantifiable result, painting a clear picture of your leadership impact.

Beyond Leadership: Comprehensive Resume Strategies

While showcasing leadership is vital, a well-rounded resume encompasses various elements.

Resume Summary/Objective: Start with a compelling introduction that encapsulates your skills, experiences, and what you aim to achieve in your next role.

Reverse Chronological Order: List your experiences from the most recent to the oldest, providing a clear trajectory of your professional growth.

Quantify Accomplishments: Use numbers to make your achievements tangible. Whether it's sales increased, costs reduced, or people managed, numbers provide scale and impact.

Tailor Your Resume: Customise your resume for each application. Align your skills and experiences with the job description, using keywords to pass Applicant Tracking Systems (ATS).

Proofread: Errors can detract significantly from your professionalism. Diligent proofreading ensures that your resume is flawless.

Additional Tips for a Standout Resume

Conciseness and Clarity: Keep your resume concise and to the point. Avoid jargon and overly complex language.

Professional Formatting: Use a clean, professional format with a readable font, appropriate margins, and strategic use of white space.

PDF Format: Save and send your resume as a PDF to preserve formatting across different devices and platforms.

Your resume is a crucial tool in your job search arsenal. By incorporating leadership-driven action verbs and following strategic resume-writing advice, you can craft a document that not only showcases your past achievements but also your potential as a future leader. Remember, a resume is not just a record of your professional history; it's a narrative of your career trajectory and a testament to your potential. Make it count.

Mastering the Interview Process as a University Graduate

"An interview is a two-way street where both parties are evaluating a fit; approach it with confidence, knowing that the interviewer is also being tested."

Navigating the transition from academia to the professional world is a pivotal moment for university graduates. The job interview, a critical step in this journey, is an opportunity to showcase your skills, experiences, and potential to prospective employers. This chapter provides a comprehensive guide on preparing for interviews and handling common questions, blending the provided material with additional insights and data.

Section 1: Preparing for the Interview

Research the Company

Understanding the company's history, products, services, and culture is crucial. Utilise the company's website, social media, and news articles to gather information. This knowledge not only helps tailor your responses but also demonstrates your genuine interest in the organisation.

Practice Common Interview Questions

Familiarity with frequently asked questions enables you to articulate clear, concise responses. Practice questions like "Tell me about yourself" and "Why are you interested in this position?" to refine your answers. Role-playing with a peer or mentor can provide constructive feedback and enhance your delivery.

Highlight Skills and Experience

Leverage academic projects, internships, volunteer work, and extracurricular activities to discuss relevant skills and experiences. Reflect on challenges you've overcome, contributions to teams, and the skills you've developed, such as leadership, problem-solving, and time management.

Dress Professionally

First impressions are lasting. Dressing professionally—appropriate to the company's culture—signals respect and seriousness about the position. This doesn't necessarily mean a suit and tie but clean, neat, and suitable attire for the work environment.

Display Confidence and Enthusiasm

Confidence and enthusiasm are infectious. They reflect your readiness and eagerness for the role. Maintain eye contact, smile, and express your excitement about the opportunity and your capabilities.

Inquire

Asking insightful questions at the interview's conclusion shows your interest and that you've done your homework. Inquire about the role, company culture, and next steps, demonstrating your proactive approach.

Section 2: Handling Common Interview Questions

Tell Me About Yourself

This open-ended question is an opportunity to highlight your journey, key achievements, and how they align with the role. Craft a succinct narrative that connects your academic experiences, internships, and personal qualities to the job you're applying for.

Why Are You Interested in This Position?

Discuss your passion for the field, the company's mission, and how the role aligns with your career aspirations. Highlight specific aspects of the company or position that excite you, showing your informed interest.

Strengths and Weaknesses

Identify strengths that are relevant to the job and share examples of how you've leveraged them. When discussing weaknesses, focus on areas of growth and how you're actively working to improve, demonstrating self-awareness and a commitment to personal development.

Salary Expectations

Research industry standards for similar roles to provide a well-informed range. Be open to negotiation, emphasising your interest in the role and the company over the starting salary.

Career Goals

Share your career aspirations in a way that demonstrates ambition while aligning with the company's trajectory. Show how the role fits into your long-term career plans, indicating your interest in growing with the company.

Biggest Challenges

Discuss a significant challenge, the strategies you used to overcome it, and what you learned. This question allows you to showcase your problem-solving skills and resilience.

Why Should We Hire You?

This is your moment to shine. Highlight your unique skills, experiences, and the value you bring to the team. Demonstrate how your background makes you a perfect fit for the role and how you can contribute to the company's success.

Additional Questions

Be prepared to discuss the company's mission and vision, industry trends, teamwork, working under pressure, feedback, and professional development. These questions assess your fit within the company culture and your professional ethos.

Section 3: Additional Tips for Fresh Graduates

Acknowledge the lack of extensive work experience while emphasising eagerness to learn. Highlight transferable skills from academic and extracurricular activities, showcasing adaptability and potential. Maintain a positive and enthusiastic demeanour, demonstrating your readiness to embark on your career journey.

The job interview is a critical gateway for university graduates entering the workforce. By thoroughly preparing, practising, and presenting yourself authentically, you can navigate this challenge successfully. Remember, each interview is a learning opportunity, paving the way to your professional future. Good luck!

Mastering Interview Preparation and Body Language for University Students

"Mastering body language in an interview can bridge the gap between your words and your worth."

Entering the professional world as a university student can be a daunting journey, with the interview process being one of the most pivotal steps towards securing your dream job. While your resume might get you through the door, how you present yourself and your body language can significantly influence the interviewer's perception of you. This chapter aims to guide university students on how to prepare for interviews, focusing on grooming and body language, ensuring they project confidence, professionalism, and approachability.

The Power of Body Language

Body language speaks volumes before you even utter a word. It's the unspoken dialogue that can set the tone for your interview. Positive body language can make you appear confident, engaged, and the right fit for the company culture.

Positive Body Language Tips

Sit Up Straight and Make Eye Contact: This signals confidence and engagement. It shows you're attentive and interested in the conversation.

Smile Genuinely: Smiling makes you appear approachable and friendly, creating a positive atmosphere during the interview.

Nod and Lean In Slightly: Nodding in agreement and leaning in shows you are actively listening and value what the interviewer is saying.

Keep Your Arms Uncrossed: Open body language indicates that you are receptive and open-minded.

Use Gestures Wisely: Controlled gestures can emphasise your points and make your communication more dynamic.

Avoid Fidgeting: Stay calm and composed. Fidgeting can detract from your message by suggesting nervousness.

Breathe Deeply: It helps in maintaining composure and reducing anxiety.

Common Body Language Mistakes

Crossing Your Arms: May suggest defensiveness or a closed-off attitude.

Avoiding Eye Contact: Can be interpreted as disinterest or lack of confidence.

Slouching: Projects a lack of energy or professionalism.

Fiddling with Objects: Indicates anxiety and detracts from your credibility.

Tapping or Drumming Fingers: Signals impatience or nervousness.

Grooming Yourself for Success

First impressions are crucial, and your appearance plays a significant role in how you're perceived by your potential employer.
Grooming Tips

Hygiene is Fundamental: Ensure you're showered, use deodorant, and have fresh breath.

Neat Hair and Nails: Your hair should be tidy, and nails should be clean and trimmed.

Subtle Makeup (if applicable):   Opt for a natural look to enhance your features without overwhelming.

Dress Appropriately: Wear professional attire that fits the company's culture and the job role.

Minimise Accessories and Fragrances: Keep jewellery and perfume/cologne to a subtle level to avoid distractions.

Additional Grooming Advice

Do a Dress Rehearsal: Test your interview outfit and grooming the day before to ensure everything is in order and you're comfortable with your appearance.

Seek Feedback: A second opinion can provide insights into aspects you might have overlooked.

Stay Relaxed: Nervousness can be managed with deep breaths and a positive mindset.

Mastering the art of body language and grooming for an interview can significantly enhance your chances of making a lasting impression. By incorporating these tips, university students can approach interviews with greater confidence and poise. Remember, preparation is key—not just in anticipating questions but also in how you present yourself. Through deliberate practice and mindfulness about your body language and grooming, you can communicate your readiness and eagerness to embark on your professional journey.

Leveraging Video Resumes and AI in Your Job Search

"Video resumes allow you to showcase your unique story and skills beyond traditional constraints. In a tech-driven recruitment landscape, authenticity and preparation are your keys to standing out and seizing new opportunities."

In the digital age, the job application process has evolved significantly, and video resumes have emerged as a powerful tool for candidates to showcase their skills and personality beyond the constraints of a traditional paper resume. This chapter delves into how university students can craft effective video resumes and explores the role of artificial intelligence (AI) in the recruitment process, offering insights into how technology is used to screen candidates.

Crafting an Effective Video Resume

1. Scripting Your Story

Start by writing a concise script that highlights your strengths, achievements, and the unique qualities you bring to the table. This script is your roadmap, ensuring that you cover all essential points without veering off track. Remember, authenticity and clarity are key; your script should sound natural and reflect your genuine self.

2. Recording Essentials

Choose a quiet, well-lit space for recording to ensure that you are clearly seen and heard. Professional attire is recommended, as it reflects your seriousness and professionalism. Even if the industry you're targeting has a more relaxed dress code, erring on the side of formality can never hurt.

3. Visual and Audio Quality

Invest in a good microphone and consider using a tripod or stabiliser to avoid shaky footage. These technical aspects play a significant role in making your video resume look and sound professional. Additionally, editing your video to cut out unnecessary parts can make your message more impactful.

4. Engaging Presentation

Your presentation should exude confidence and enthusiasm. Demonstrate your excitement for the potential opportunity and confidence in your abilities. Keep your video concise, aiming for a length of 2-3 minutes, to maintain the viewer's attention.

5. Feedback and Refinement

Before finalising your video, seek feedback from peers, mentors, or professionals in your field. Constructive criticism can provide invaluable insights into how your video is perceived and what improvements can be made.

The Role of AI in Screening Video Resumes

The use of AI in screening candidates is becoming increasingly common. AI-powered systems can analyse video resumes for various elements, including speech patterns, keywords, and even non-verbal cues, to assess a candidate's suitability for a role.

AI and Keyword Analysis

Integrating relevant keywords into your video script can significantly increase your visibility. AI algorithms often scan for specific keywords related to the job description to identify potentially suitable candidates. Tailor your video resume to include these keywords naturally within your presentation.

Non-Verbal Cues and AI

AI technology can also interpret non-verbal cues, such as facial expressions and body language, to gauge a candidate's confidence, enthusiasm, and suitability for the role. Being aware of your body language and ensuring it aligns with your verbal message can enhance your video resume's effectiveness.

Personalisation and Authenticity

While AI plays a significant role in the initial screening process, the human element remains crucial. Personalise your video resume to the specific job and company you're applying for, highlighting how your skills and experiences align with the company's needs and culture. Authenticity is key; let your personality shine through to make a memorable impression.

Video resumes represent a unique opportunity to stand out in the job market. By combining careful preparation, technical quality, and personal authenticity, you can create a compelling video resume that captures the attention of potential employers. Simultaneously, understanding the role of AI in the recruitment process can help you optimise your video resume to pass through initial screenings and land that all-important interview. As technology continues to evolve, staying abreast of these advancements and integrating them into your job search strategy will be crucial for success.

Enhancing Your Resume Through Leadership and Engagement on Campus

"Leadership and active participation in campus activities are more than resume builders; they are the stepping stones that transform academic knowledge into real-world expertise, setting you apart in a competitive job market."

In the competitive job market of today, university students must go beyond academic achievements to distinguish themselves. Leadership and active participation in campus activities are invaluable for showcasing your capabilities to potential employers. This chapter delves into how you can leverage these opportunities to enhance your resume and stand out as a job applicant.

Embracing Leadership Roles

Leadership experience is highly regarded by employers as it demonstrates your ability to take initiative, manage projects, and work collaboratively with others. Here are ways to display leadership on campus:

Student Government: Involvement in student government is a prime avenue for honing your leadership skills. It provides a platform to work on issues that impact the student body, learn about governance, and participate in decision-making processes. Leadership roles within student government can significantly bolster your resume, showing potential employers your capability to handle responsibility and navigate complex organisational dynamics.

Clubs and Organisations: Joining clubs and organisations related to your field of interest not only enriches your university experience but also offers leadership opportunities. Whether you become the president of a club, lead a committee, or organise events, these roles demonstrate your commitment, team coordination skills, and ability to achieve goals.

Contributing to Your Community

Giving back to your community through volunteering or service projects is another way to develop and showcase your leadership skills. It reflects your ability to empathise, initiate change, and commit to causes beyond personal gain. Highlight these experiences on your resume to show a well-rounded character and a strong sense of social responsibility.

Gaining Practical Experience

Research: Participating in research projects allows you to gain in-depth knowledge in your field. Leadership roles in research can include leading a research team, managing a lab, or coordinating research projects. These experiences underscore your analytical skills, ability to work in a team, and commitment to advancing knowledge.

Internships: Internships offer real-world experience and networking opportunities. Taking on leadership roles or projects during an internship can significantly enhance your resume. It shows that you can apply your academic knowledge in practical settings and are proactive in taking on challenges.

Teaching Assistantships and Tutoring: These roles allow you to develop leadership and mentoring skills. As a teaching assistant or tutor, you're not just imparting knowledge; you're also learning to communicate effectively, manage time, and inspire others. These experiences are invaluable for any career path, demonstrating your leadership potential and dedication to helping others succeed.

Tips for Maximising Your Campus Involvement

Start Early: Engage in campus activities from your first year to build a rich portfolio of experiences.

Seek Advice: Consult with advisers or career services to identify opportunities that align with your career goals.

Diversify Your Involvement: Participate in a variety of activities to develop a broad skill set and discover new interests.

Take on Leadership Roles: Actively seek leadership positions or propose new initiatives within organisations.

Align with Your Career Goals: Choose activities that are relevant to your field of study to develop industry-specific skills.

Your time at university is a unique opportunity to explore interests, develop new skills, and demonstrate leadership.

By strategically choosing and participating in campus activities, you can create a compelling resume that showcases your readiness for the professional world. Remember, the experiences you gain during this time are not just resume builders; they are stepping stones to your future career. Engage deeply, lead with purpose, and seize the opportunities that university life offers to prepare yourself for a successful transition to the workforce.

Twenty Powerful Pro Tips For Young Professionals

"Your personal growth hinges more on who you choose to listen to than on who merely offers advice."

As you step into your career, here is my final list of pro tips to help you thrive and excel:

1. Define Your Vision: Write down the vision for your life and what you want to be known for when you leave this world. Let this vision guide your decisions and actions.

2. Health First: Maintain your physical health and guard your mental health zealously.

3. Learn to Sell Early: Whether it's an idea, a product, or yourself, mastering the art of selling is crucial.

4. Master Business Communication: Proficiency in English, the global language of business, is essential. Learn to communicate effectively and connect with others.

5. Build a Strong Support Network: Surround yourself with the best people you know. Leave your ego at the door and learn from them.

6. Choose Your Partner Wisely: Marriage is a pivotal decision. Don't rely solely on emotions; consider compatibility and long-term goals.

7. Understand Money: Embrace financial literacy. Avoid comparisons and the herd mentality. Educate yourself on investments and let your money work for you.

8. Network Relentlessly: Cultivate and protect your network. Networking is invaluable—invest in it diligently.

9. Be Indispensable to Your Boss: Take on tasks others avoid. Become the go-to person for your boss by mastering skills they lack.

10. Master Storytelling: Create compelling narratives around your ideas and experiences. Effective storytelling can set you apart.

11. Stay Curious: Always ask questions and maintain a high level of energy in all interactions. Curiosity drives innovation and learning.

12. Be an Information Sponge: Read extensively, listen to podcasts, and stay informed. Use critical thinking to connect the dots and identify patterns.

13. Think Long-Term: Always consider the strategic long-term view, except in immediate emergencies.

14. Invest in Yourself: Continuously learn, unlearn, and relearn. Personal growth is your greatest asset.

15. Practice Forgiveness and Kindness: Let go of past grievances. Be kind to others and give them the benefit of the doubt. Start by forgiving yourself.

16. Family Is What Makes It All Worth It: Enjoy your family and cherish them. Celebrate your successes with them.

17. Conquer Fear: Whenever you see people and markets fearful; take it as a signal for windfall opportunities and look for them.

18. Deep Domain Knowledge: Have at least one industry that you have deep domain knowledge in and are acknowledged as a thought leader.

19. The Power of No: Learn to say no, whoever it is on the other side and however tempting the offer.

20. I Don't Know: Approach every situation, adversary and conversation with an "I don't know" attitude. This will force you to seek information and knowledge.

These tips are your toolkit for a successful and fulfilling career. Embrace them, and you'll navigate your professional journey with confidence and purpose.

Author's Note

As you hold this book, you are embarking on a journey into the depths of human resilience and leadership. Throughout history, our heroes and role models—whether mythical gods or towering figures like Martin Luther King, Mahatma Gandhi, and Steve Jobs—have possessed timeless qualities that have set them apart. They have not only inspired their contemporaries but continue to influence generations long after their time. This book explores the essence of what makes these individuals extraordinary. What traits, skills, and habits did they cultivate to succeed against all odds? Is there a universal lesson embedded in their stories that we can apply in our own lives?

My quest to answer these questions began by observing leaders who often struggle with conventional self-help books and mentorship programmes that promise quick fixes but fail to deliver lasting impact. I watched the trials and frustrations of young people on university campuses and in workplaces, wrestling with the disconnect between education and the actual demands of the job market. This sparked a deep investigation into the lives of our greatest role models, stripping away the myth and legend to uncover the core skills that can stand the test of time.

This investigation revealed the "Halo Skills"—five essential skills that have not only shaped great leaders through the ages but are increasingly relevant in today's cluttered and fast-paced world. Before diving into these skills, I provide a context of the current job market landscape to help you understand the dynamics at play as we move into Industry 4.0 and beyond.

The jobs of the future are largely unknown, but insights into emerging trends can equip you with the necessary tools to navigate this uncertainty. By understanding these dynamics, you can better prepare yourself to select a career path that is not only relevant but also fulfilling.

For those of you standing at the threshold of your careers, the challenge is real. The pace of change in the job market often renders traditional education inadequate, leaving many graduates feeling unprepared and overwhelmed. In these pages, I offer strategies to enhance job readiness from the ground up, tailored to bridge the gap between academic preparation and professional requirements. Programmes like the groundbreaking Orbit Job Readiness programme exemplify the kind of innovative approaches that can accelerate your readiness and vastly improve your chances of securing meaningful employment.

This book is a culmination of lessons learned from a diverse range of experiences and individuals who have enriched my life. I am profoundly grateful to my family, friends, and colleagues, from whom I have learned more than I could ever acknowledge. Your unwavering support and respect have been my strength. Equally, I owe a heartfelt thank you to those who have challenged me; your dissent has been invaluable, forcing me to reflect and grow in ways I never expected.

As we move forward together through these pages, I hope to offer you not just insights but also inspiration. May this book serve as a guide and a companion in your professional journey, helping you to navigate the complexities of modern careers with confidence and purpose. Here's to embarking on this new adventure—to learning, growing, and succeeding. All the best in your endeavours.